Introduction

The Science Coordination Group has been set up with the aim of producing specialised revision material for National Curriculum Science.
This is one of a set of six books which provide concise coverage of the National Curriculum Key Stage 4 syllabus for *GCSE Double Science*.
They are ideally suited to all syllabuses produced by the main Examination Boards for GCSE Double Science, both Coordinated and Modular.

Throughout these books there is constant emphasis on the inescapable need *to keep learning the basic facts*. This simple message is hammered home without compromise and without remorse, and whilst this traditionally brutal philosophy may not be quite in line with some other approaches to education, we still rather like it.   But only because it works.

Contents

Section One — Classifying Materials

Solids, Liquids and Gases 1
Changes of State 2
Brownian Motion and Diffusion 4
Atoms 6
Atomic Number and Mass Number 7
Electron Shells and Ionic Bonding 8
Ionic Bonding and Covalent Bonding 9
Ionic Substances 10
Covalent Substances: Two Kinds 11
Elements, Compounds and Mixtures 12
Separation Techniques 13
Separation Techniques 14
Common Tests and Hazard Symbols 15
Revision Summary for Section One 16

Section Two — Earth Materials

Crude Oil 17
Fractional Distillation of Crude Oil 18
Using Hydrocarbons 19
Cracking Hydrocarbons 20
Alkanes and Alkenes 21
Polymers and Plastics 22
Metal Ores From the Ground 23
Extracting Iron — the Blast Furnace 24
Purifying Copper by Electrolysis 25
Extracting Aluminium — Electrolysis 26
Uses of The Three Common Metals 28
Four Uses Of Limestone 29
Making Ammonia: The Haber Process 30
Using Ammonia to Make Fertilisers 31
Revision Summary for Section Two 32

Section Three — Equations

Nine Types of Chemical Change 33
Balancing Equations 34
Electrolysis and The Half Equations 35
Relative Formula Mass 36
Calculating Percentage Mass 37
Revision Summary for Section Three 38

Section Four — Air and Rock

Today's Atmosphere 39
The Evolution of the Atmosphere 40
Man-made Atmospheric Problems 42
The Carbon Cycle 44
Weathering and the Water Cycle 45

The Three Different Types of Rocks 46
Sedimentary Rocks 47
Metamorphic Rocks 48
Igneous Rocks 49
The Earth's Structure 50
Evidence for Plate Tectonics 51
Plate Boundaries 52
Revision Summary For Section Four 54

Section Five — Periodic Trends

A Brief History of The Periodic Table 55
The Periodic Table 56
Electron Arrangements 57
Group O — The Noble Gases 58
Group I — The Alkali Metals 59
Reactions of the Alkali Metals 60
Group VII — The Halogens 62
Reactions of The Halogens 63
Industrial Salt 64
Uses of Halogens and Salt Products 65
Acids and Alkalis 66
Acids Reacting With Metals 67
Acids with Oxides and Hydroxides 68
Acids With Carbonates and Ammonia 69
Metals 70
Non-Metals 71
The Reactivity Series of Metals 72
Reactivity of Metals 73
Metal Displacement Reactions 74
Corrosion of Metals 75
Transition Metals 76
Revision Summary for Section Five 77

Section Six — Reaction Rates

Rates of Reaction 78
Collision Theory 79
Four Experiments on Rate of Reaction 80
Catalysts 82
Biological Catalysts — Enzymes 83
Uses of Enzymes 84
Simple Reversible Reactions 85
Energy Transfer in Reactions 86
Revision Summary for Section Six 88

Answers 88
Index 89

Page References for Modular Syllabuses

NEAB Double Award Science — Modular Syllabus 1998

Module 5: Metals .... Pages: 23-28, 66-68, 70-75

Module 6: Earth Materials .... Pages: 17-22, 29, 39-43, 45-53

Module 7: Patterns of Chemical Change .... Pages: 13-15, 30-31, 36-37, 78-88

Module 8: Structures and Bonding .... Pages: 1-12, 34-35, 55-65, 76

ULEAC Double Award Science — Modular Syllabus 1998

Module 4: Chemicals and the Earth .... Pages: 23-31, 39-43, 45-53, 64-65, 70-75, 85

Module 5: Materials Chemistry .... Pages: 1-14, 34-37, 57-58, 83-84

Module 6: Chemical Patterns .... Pages: 6-7, 19-22, 55-66, 76, 78-82, 86-87

Module 10: Energy and Gravitation .... Pages: 14, 17-19
                (The rest of this module is covered in the Physics book.)

SEG Double Award Science — Modular Syllabus 1998

Module 3: Structure and Changes .... Pages: 6-7, 17-22, 55-75, 78-82

Module 5: Energy Sources .... Pages: 86-87
                (The majority of this module is covered in the Physics book.)

Module 6: Vital Exchanges .... Pages: 83-84
                (The majority of this module is covered in the Biology book.)

Module 7: Bonding and Materials .... Pages: 1-15, 30-31, 33-38, 76, 85

Module 9: Universal Changes .... Pages: 23-28, 39-54
                (The rest of this module is covered in the Physics book.)

Typesetting and Layout by The Science Coordination Group
Illustrations by Sandy Gardner e-mail: zimkit@aol.com

Consultant Editor: Paddy Gannon BSc MA

Solids, Liquids and Gases

These are known as the *three states of matter*. Make sure you know everything there is to know.

Solids have Strong Forces of Attraction

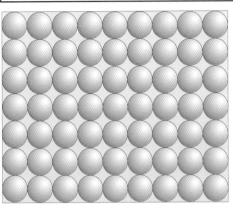

1) There are *strong forces* of *attraction* between molecules.
2) The molecules are *held* in *fixed positions* in a very regular *lattice arrangement*.
3) They *don't move* from their positions, so all solids keep a *definite shape* and *volume*, and don't flow like liquids.
4) They *vibrate* about their positions. The *hotter* the solid becomes, the *more* they *vibrate*. This causes solids to *expand* slightly when heated.
5) Solids *can't be compressed* **easily** because the molecules are already packed *very closely together*.
6) Solids are generally *very dense*.

Liquids have Moderate Forces of Attraction

1) There is *some force* of *attraction* between the molecules.
2) The molecules are *free to move* past each other, but they do tend to *stick together*.
3) Liquids *don't* keep a *definite shape* and will flow to *fill the bottom* of a container. But they do keep the *same volume*.
4) The molecules are *constantly* moving in *random motion*. The *hotter* the liquid becomes, the *faster* they move. This causes liquids to *expand* slightly when heated.
5) Liquids *can't be compressed* because the molecules are already packed *closely together*.
6) Liquids are *quite dense*, but not as dense as solids.

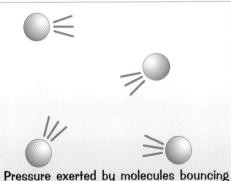

Gases have No Forces of Attraction

1) There is *no force* of *attraction* between the molecules.
2) The molecules are *free to move*. They travel in *straight lines* and only interact with each other *when they collide*.
3) Gases *don't* keep a *definite shape* or *volume* and will always *expand to fill* any container. Gases exert a *pressure* on the walls of the container.
4) The molecules are *constantly* moving in *random motion*. The *hotter* the gas becomes, the *faster* they move. When *heated*, a gas will either *expand* or its *pressure* will *increase*.
5) *Gases* can be *compressed* easily because there's *a lot of free space* between the molecules.
6) Gases all have *very low densities*.

Pressure exerted by molecules bouncing off the walls of the container.

Don't get yourself in a state about this lot, just learn it...

This is pretty basic stuff, but people still lose marks in the Exam because they don't make sure to learn all the little details really thoroughly. And there's only one way to do that: *COVER THE PAGE UP AND SCRIBBLE IT ALL DOWN FROM MEMORY*. That soon shows what you really know — and that's what you've got to do for every page. Do it now for this one, *AND KEEP TRYING UNTIL YOU CAN.*

Changes of State

CHANGES OF STATE always involve *HEAT ENERGY* going either *IN* or *OUT*.

Melting — the rigid lattice breaks down

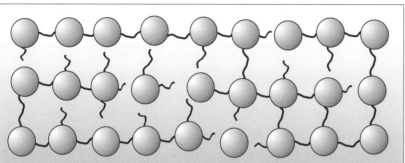

1) When a *SOLID* is *heated*, the heat energy goes *to the molecules*.

2) It makes them vibrate *more and more*.

3) Eventually *the strong forces* between the molecules (that hold them in the rigid lattice) are *overcome*, and the molecules start to *move around*. The solid has now *MELTED*.

Evaporation — the fastest molecules escape

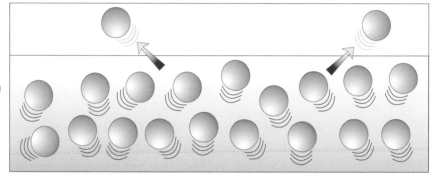

1) When a *LIQUID* is *heated*, the heat energy goes *to the molecules*, which makes them *move faster*.

2) Some molecules move *faster* than others do.

3) Fast-moving molecules *at the surface* will *overcome* the *forces of attraction* from the other molecules and *escape*. This is *EVAPORATION*.

Boiling — all molecules are fast enough to escape

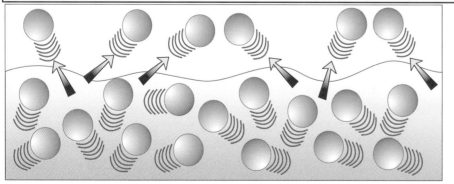

1) When the liquid gets *hot enough*, virtually *all* the molecules have *enough speed and energy* to overcome the forces and *escape each other*.

2) At this point *big bubbles of gas* form inside the liquid as the molecules *break away* from each other. This is *BOILING*.

Simmer down — this stuff's really quite easy...

There are three diagrams and just eight numbered points on this page. They wouldn't be there if you didn't need to learn them. *So learn them*. Then cover the page and scribble them all down. You have to realise this is the only way to really learn stuff properly. *And learn it you must*.

Changes of State

Heating and Cooling Graphs Have Important Flat Spots

1) When a substance is _MELTING_ or _BOILING_, all the _heat energy_ supplied is used for _breaking bonds_ rather than raising the temperature, hence the _flat spots_ in the heating graph shown here.

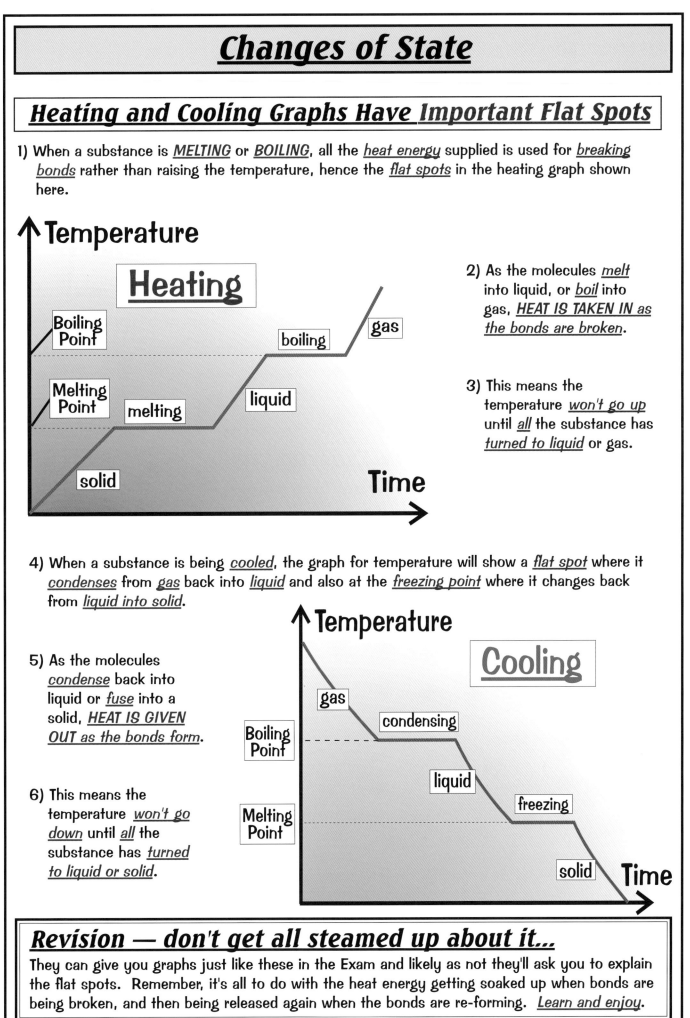

2) As the molecules _melt_ into liquid, or _boil_ into gas, _HEAT IS TAKEN IN as the bonds are broken_.

3) This means the temperature _won't go up_ until _all_ the substance has _turned to liquid_ or gas.

4) When a substance is being _cooled_, the graph for temperature will show a _flat spot_ where it _condenses_ from _gas_ back into _liquid_ and also at the _freezing point_ where it changes back from _liquid into solid_.

5) As the molecules _condense_ back into liquid or _fuse_ into a solid, _HEAT IS GIVEN OUT as the bonds form_.

6) This means the temperature _won't go down_ until _all_ the substance has _turned to liquid or solid_.

Revision — don't get all steamed up about it...

They can give you graphs just like these in the Exam and likely as not they'll ask you to explain the flat spots. Remember, it's all to do with the heat energy getting soaked up when bonds are being broken, and then being released again when the bonds are re-forming. _Learn and enjoy_.

Brownian Motion and Diffusion

Brownian Motion is Jerky Random Motion

1) _Brownian motion_ is the _jerky movement_ of _smoke_ particles, as seen through a microscope.
2) It's _caused_ by _air molecules bumping into the smoke particles_ and knocking them about.
3) The smoke particles _reflect the light_ shone onto them — they're seen as _bright specks_.
4) Brownian motion can also be seen in _pollen grains in water_, looked at through a microscope.

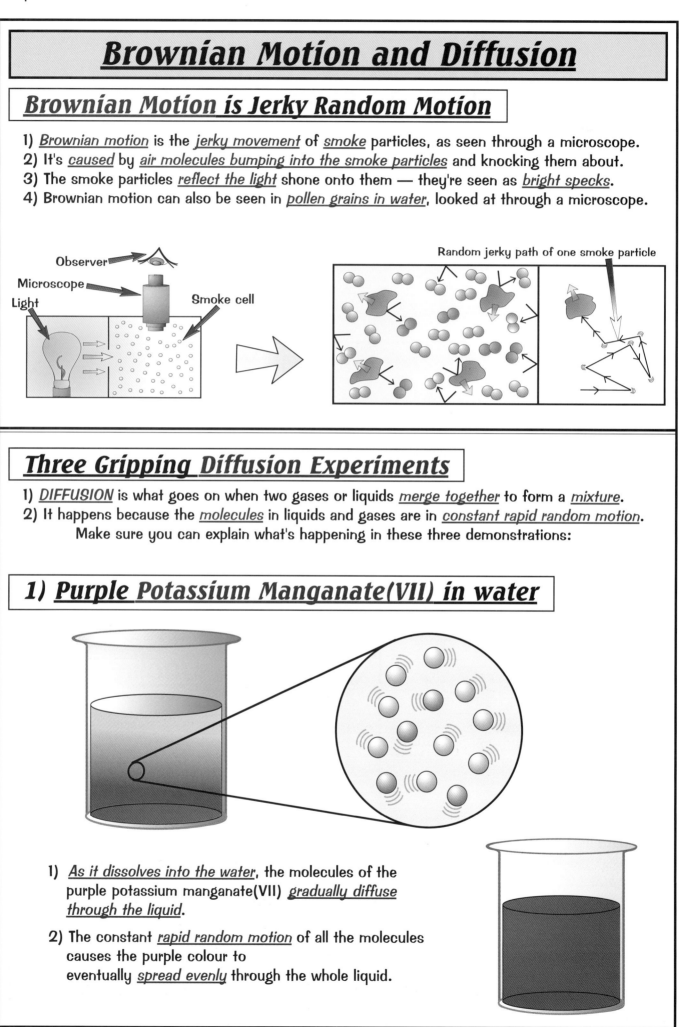

Three Gripping Diffusion Experiments

1) _DIFFUSION_ is what goes on when two gases or liquids _merge together_ to form a _mixture_.
2) It happens because the _molecules_ in liquids and gases are in _constant rapid random motion_.
   Make sure you can explain what's happening in these three demonstrations:

1) Purple Potassium Manganate(VII) in water

1) _As it dissolves into the water_, the molecules of the purple potassium manganate(VII) _gradually diffuse through the liquid_.

2) The constant _rapid random motion_ of all the molecules causes the purple colour to eventually _spread evenly_ through the whole liquid.

Brownian Motion and Diffusion

2) Good old Boring Brown Bromine

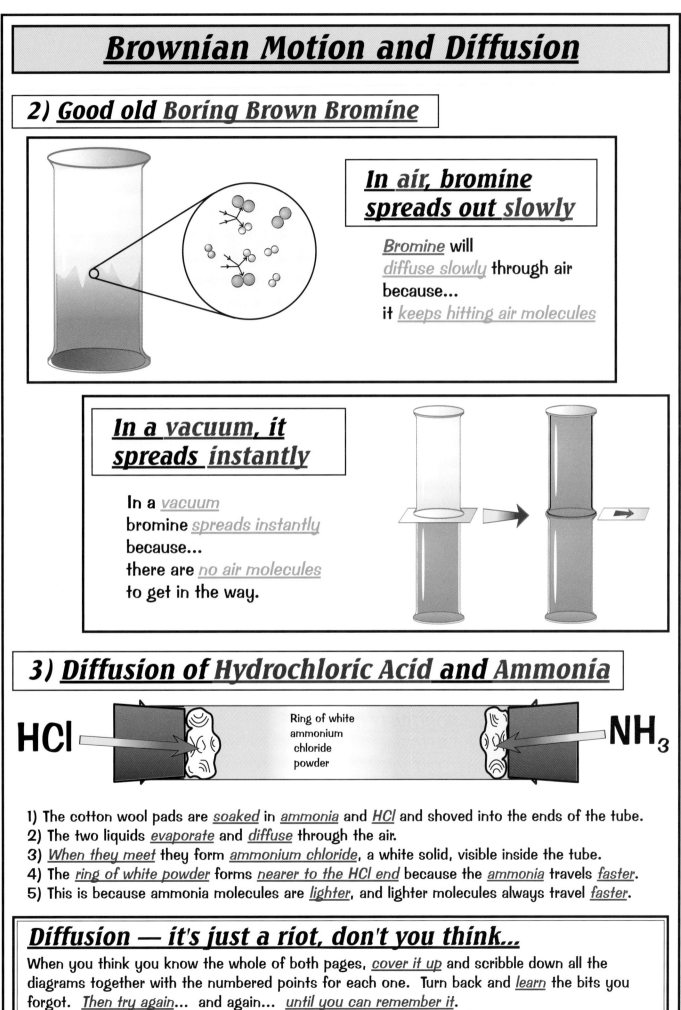

In air, bromine spreads out slowly

Bromine will
diffuse slowly through air
because...
it keeps hitting air molecules

In a vacuum, it spreads instantly

In a vacuum
bromine spreads instantly
because...
there are no air molecules
to get in the way.

3) Diffusion of Hydrochloric Acid and Ammonia

Ring of white
ammonium
chloride
powder

HCl   NH₃

1) The cotton wool pads are soaked in ammonia and HCl and shoved into the ends of the tube.
2) The two liquids evaporate and diffuse through the air.
3) When they meet they form ammonium chloride, a white solid, visible inside the tube.
4) The ring of white powder forms nearer to the HCl end because the ammonia travels faster.
5) This is because ammonia molecules are lighter, and lighter molecules always travel faster.

Diffusion — it's just a riot, don't you think...

When you think you know the whole of both pages, cover it up and scribble down all the diagrams together with the numbered points for each one. Turn back and learn the bits you forgot. Then try again... and again... until you can remember it.

Atoms

The structure of atoms is real simple. I mean, gee, there's nothing to them. Just learn and enjoy.

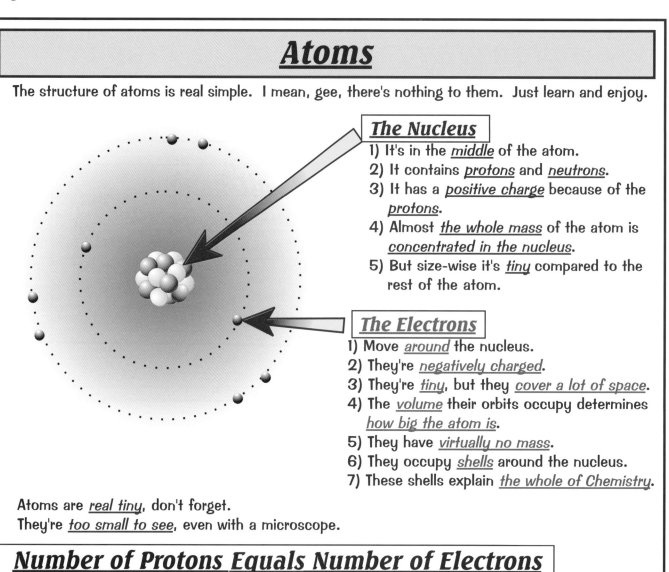

The Nucleus

1) It's in the *middle* of the atom.
2) It contains *protons* and *neutrons*.
3) It has a *positive charge* because of the *protons*.
4) Almost *the whole mass* of the atom is *concentrated in the nucleus*.
5) But size-wise it's *tiny* compared to the rest of the atom.

The Electrons

1) Move *around* the nucleus.
2) They're *negatively charged*.
3) They're *tiny*, but they *cover a lot of space*.
4) The *volume* their orbits occupy determines *how big the atom is*.
5) They have *virtually no mass*.
6) They occupy *shells* around the nucleus.
7) These shells explain *the whole of Chemistry*.

Atoms are *real tiny*, don't forget.
They're *too small to see*, even with a microscope.

Number of Protons Equals Number of Electrons

1) Neutral atoms have *no charge* overall.
2) The *charge* on the *electrons* is *the same size* as the charge on the *protons* but *opposite*.
3) This means the *number of protons* always *equals* the *number of electrons* in a *neutral atom*.
4) If some electrons are *added or removed*, the atom becomes *charged* and is then an *ION*.
5) The number of neutrons isn't fixed but is usually *just a bit higher* than the number of protons.

Know Your Particles

PROTONS are *HEAVY* and *POSITIVELY CHARGED*
NEUTRONS are *HEAVY* and *NEUTRAL*
ELECTRONS are *Tiny* and *NEGATIVELY CHARGED*

PARTICLE	MASS	CHARGE
Proton	1	+1
Neutron	1	0
Electron	$\frac{1}{2000}$	- 1

Basic Atom facts — they don't take up much space...

This stuff on atoms should be permanently engraved in the minds of everyone.
I don't understand how people can get through the day without knowing this stuff, really I don't.
LEARN IT NOW, and watch as the Universe unfolds and reveals its timeless mysteries to you...

Atomic Number and Mass Number

Come on. These are just *two simple numbers* for goodness' sake.
It just can't be that difficult to remember what they tell you about an atom.

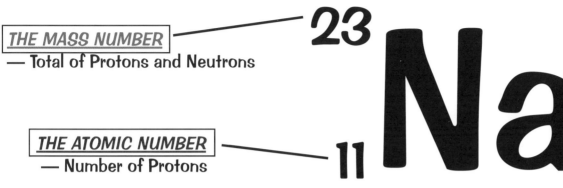

THE MASS NUMBER
— Total of Protons and Neutrons

THE ATOMIC NUMBER
— Number of Protons

POINTS TO NOTE
1) The *atomic number* tells you how many *protons* there are.
2) This *also* tells you how many *electrons* there are.
3) To get the number of *neutrons* — just *subtract* the *atomic number* from the *mass number*.
4) The *mass number* is always the *biggest* number. It tells you the relative mass of the atom.
5) The *mass* number is always *roughly double* the *atomic* number.
6) Which means there's about the *same* number of protons as neutrons in any nucleus.

Isotopes are the same except for an extra neutron or two

A favourite trick Exam question: "Explain what is meant by the term *Isotope*"
The trick is that it's impossible to explain what one isotope is. Nice of them that isn't it!
You have to outsmart them and always start your answer "ISOTOPES ARE...
LEARN THE DEFINITION:

> **ISOTOPES ARE:** different atomic forms of the **same element**, which have the **SAME** number of **PROTONS** but a **DIFFERENT** number of **NEUTRONS**.

1) The upshot is: isotopes must have *the same atomic number* but *different mass numbers*.
2) *If* they had *different* atomic numbers, they'd be *different elements altogether*.
3) A very popular pair of isotopes are *carbon-12* and *carbon-14*.

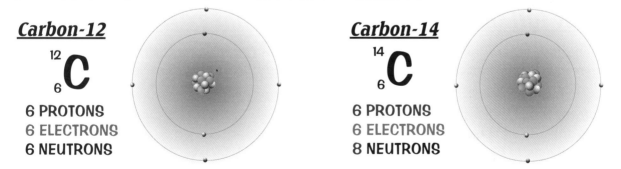

Carbon-12
$^{12}_{6}C$
6 PROTONS
6 ELECTRONS
6 NEUTRONS

Carbon-14
$^{14}_{6}C$
6 PROTONS
6 ELECTRONS
8 NEUTRONS

The number of electrons decides the chemistry of the element. If the atomic number is the same, then the number of protons is the same, so the number of electrons is the same, so the chemistry is the same. The different number of neutrons in the nucleus doesn't affect the chemical behaviour at all.

Learn what those blinking numbers mean...

There really isn't that much information on this page — three definitions, a couple of diagrams and a dozen or so extra details. All you gotta do is *READ IT*, *LEARN IT*, *COVER THE PAGE* and *SCRIBBLE IT ALL DOWN AGAIN*. Smile and enjoy.

Electron Shells and Ionic Bonding

The fact that electrons occupy "shells" around the nucleus is what causes the whole of chemistry.
Remember that, and watch how it applies to each bit of it. It's ace.

Electron Shell Rules:

1) Electrons always occupy _SHELLS_ or _ENERGY LEVELS_.
2) The _LOWEST_ energy levels are _ALWAYS FILLED FIRST_.
3) Only _a certain number_ of electrons are allowed in each shell:
   1st shell: 2
   2nd Shell: 8
   3rd Shell: 8
4) Atoms are much _HAPPIER_ when they have _FULL electron shells_.
5) In most atoms the _OUTER SHELL_ is _NOT FULL_ and this makes the atom want to _REACT_.

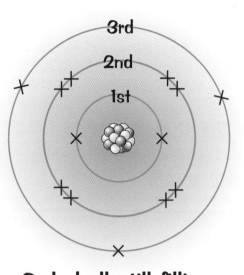

3rd shell still filling

A shell with just one electron is well keen to get rid...

1) _All_ the atoms over at the _left hand side_ of the periodic table, such as _sodium, potassium, calcium_ etc. have just _one or two electrons_ in their outer shell.
2) And basically they're _pretty keen to get shot of them_, because then they'll only have _full shells_ left, which is how they _like_ it.
3) So given half a chance they do get rid, and that leaves the atom as an _ION_ instead.
4) Now ions aren't the kind of things that sit around quietly watching the world go by.
5) They tend to _leap_ at the first passing ion with an _opposite charge_ and stick to it like glue.

A nearly full shell is well keen to get that extra electron...

1) On the _other side_ of the periodic table, the elements in _Group Six_ and _Group Seven_, such as _oxygen_ and _chlorine_ have outer shells which are _nearly full_.
2) They're obviously pretty keen to _gain_ that _extra one or two electrons_ to fill the shell up.
3) When they do of course they become _IONS_, you know, not the kind of things to sit around, and before you know it, _POP_, they've latched onto the atom (ion) that gave up the electron a moment earlier. The reaction of _sodium and chlorine_ is a _classic case_ as shown on the next page:

Full Shells — it's the name of the game, pal...

There's quite a lot of words on this page but only to hammer home two very basic points:
1) Electrons have shells — with rules.
2) Some atoms like to lose them, some like to gain them. _LEARN ALL THE HIGHLIGHTED BITS._

SECTION ONE — CLASSIFYING MATERIALS

Ionic Bonding and Covalent Bonding

In *IONIC BONDING*, atoms *lose or gain electrons* to form *charged particles* (ions) which are then *strongly attracted* to one another (the attraction of opposite charges, + and –).
In *COVALENT BONDING* electrons are *shared*, not swapped.

Ionic Bonding — Swapping Electrons

1) *Ionic bonding* is easy to understand.
2) *Electrons jump* from one one atom to another and they both end up with *full electron shells*.
3) They then get *attracted* to each other because they have *opposite charges*.

1) The *sodium* atom *gives up* its *outer electron* and becomes an Na⁺ ion.

2) The *chlorine* atom *picks up* the *spare electron* and becomes a Cl⁻ ion.

3) Then, before you know it...

POP!

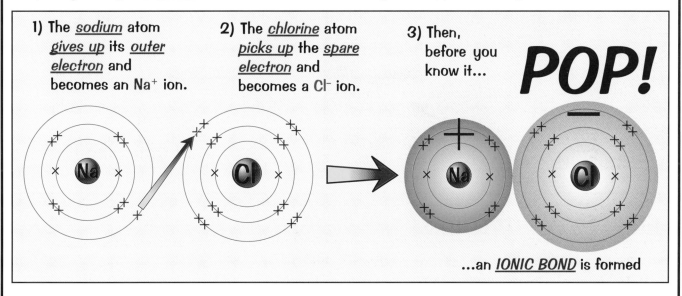

...an *IONIC BOND* is formed

Covalent Bonds — Sharing Electrons

1) *Sometimes* atoms prefer to make *COVALENT BONDS* by *sharing electrons* with other atoms.
2) This way *both atoms* feel that they have *a full outer shell*, and that makes them happy.
3) *Each covalent bond* provides *one extra shared electron* for each atom.
4) Each atom involved has to make *enough covalent bonds* to *fill up* its outer shell.

Hydrogen Molecule, H_2

Shared electrons

Water Molecule, H_2O

Full Shells — you just can't beat them...

LEARN the diagram for the formation of ionic bonds, with its three steps.
LEARN the four numbered points about covalent bonds and the two examples.
Then turn over and scribble it all down again. *All from memory of course.*

Ionic Substances

Simple Ions — Groups 1 & 2 and 6 & 7

1) The elements that _most readily form ions_ are those in Groups 1, 2, 6 and 7.
2) _Group 1 and 2 elements_ are _metals_ and they _lose_ electrons to form _+ve ions_ or _cations_.
3) _Group 6 and 7 elements_ are _non-metals_. They _gain_ electrons to form _–ve ions_ or _anions_.
4) Make sure you know these easy ones:

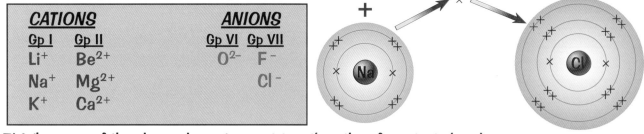

CATIONS		ANIONS	
Gp I	**Gp II**	**Gp VI**	**Gp VII**
Li^+	Be^{2+}	O^{2-}	F^-
Na^+	Mg^{2+}		Cl^-
K^+	Ca^{2+}		

5) When any of the above elements _react together_, they form _ionic bonds_.
6) Only elements at _opposite sides_ of the periodic table will form ionic bonds, e.g. Na and Cl, where one of them becomes a _CATION_ (+ve) and one becomes an _ANION_ (–ve).

Remember, the + and – charges we talk about, e.g. Na^+ for sodium, just tell you what type of ion the atom WILL FORM in a chemical reaction. In sodium _metal_ there are _only neutral sodium atoms_, Na. The Na^+ ions _will only appear_ if the sodium metal _reacts_ with something like water or chlorine.

Giant Ionic Structures don't melt easily, but when they do...

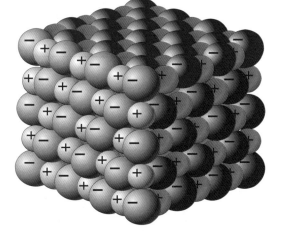

1) _Ionic bonds_ always produce _giant ionic structures_.
2) The ions form a _closely packed regular_ arrangement, as shown.
3) There are _very strong chemical bonds_ between _all_ the ions.
4) A single crystal of salt is _one giant ionic lattice_, which is why salt crystals tend to be cuboid in shape:

1) They have _High melting points and boiling points_
due to the _very strong chemical bonds_ between _all the ions_ in the giant structure.

2) They _Dissolve to form solutions that conduct electricity_
When dissolved the ions _separate_ and are all _free to move_ in the solution, so obviously they'll _carry electric current_.

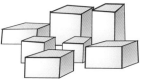

Dissolved in Water

Melted

3) They _Conduct electricity when molten_
When it _melts_, the ions are _free to move_ and they'll carry electric current.

Giant Structures — like salt crystals? You betcha...
LEARN which atoms form 1+, 1–, 2+ and 2– ions, and why (see P. 8). Then learn all the features of ionic solids. When you think you know it all, _cover the page_ and start scribbling to see what you do know. Then look back, _learn the bits you missed_, and _try again_. And again.

Covalent Substances: Two Kinds

Substances formed from _covalent bonds_ can either be _simple molecules_ or _giant structures_.

Simple Molecular Substances are Kinda Mushy

1) The atoms form _very strong covalent bonds_ to form _small molecules_ of several atoms.
2) By contrast, the forces of attraction _between_ these molecules are _very weak_.
3) The _result_ of these _feeble inter-molecular forces_ is that the _melting-_ and _boiling-points_ are _very low_, because the molecules are _easily parted_ from each other.
4) Most molecular substances are _gases or liquids_ at room temperature.
5) Molecular substances _don't conduct electricity_, simply because there are _no ions_.
6) They _don't dissolve in water_, usually.
7) You can usually tell a molecular substance just from its _physical state_, which is always kinda "_mushy_" — i.e. _liquid_ or _gas_ or an _easily-melted solid_.

Very weak inter-molecular forces

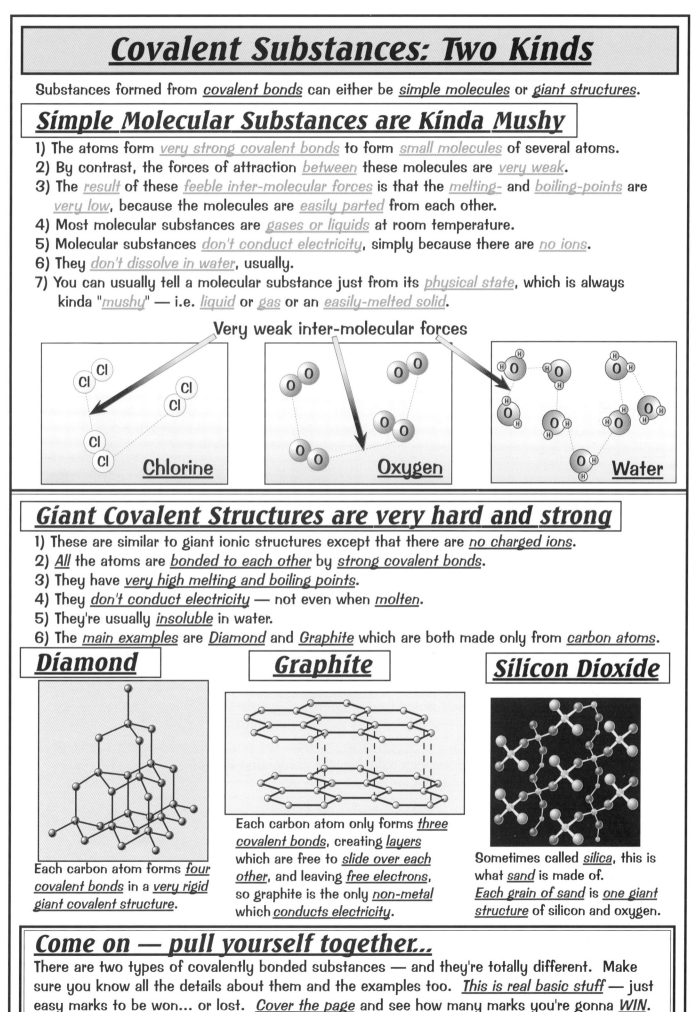

Chlorine   Oxygen   Water

Giant Covalent Structures are very hard and strong

1) These are similar to giant ionic structures except that there are _no charged ions_.
2) _All_ the atoms are _bonded to each other_ by _strong covalent bonds_.
3) They have _very high melting and boiling points_.
4) They _don't conduct electricity_ — not even when _molten_.
5) They're usually _insoluble_ in water.
6) The _main examples_ are _Diamond_ and _Graphite_ which are both made only from _carbon atoms_.

Diamond

Each carbon atom forms _four covalent bonds_ in a _very rigid giant covalent structure_.

Graphite

Each carbon atom only forms _three covalent bonds_, creating _layers_ which are free to _slide over each other_, and leaving _free electrons_, so graphite is the only _non-metal_ which _conducts electricity_.

Silicon Dioxide

Sometimes called _silica_, this is what _sand_ is made of.
Each grain of sand is _one giant structure_ of silicon and oxygen.

Come on — pull yourself together...

There are two types of covalently bonded substances — and they're totally different. Make sure you know all the details about them and the examples too. _This is real basic stuff_ — just easy marks to be won... or lost. _Cover the page_ and see how many marks you're gonna _WIN_.

Elements, Compounds and Mixtures

You'd better be sure you know the _subtle difference_ between these.

Elements consist of one type of atom only

Quite a lot of everyday substances are _elements_:

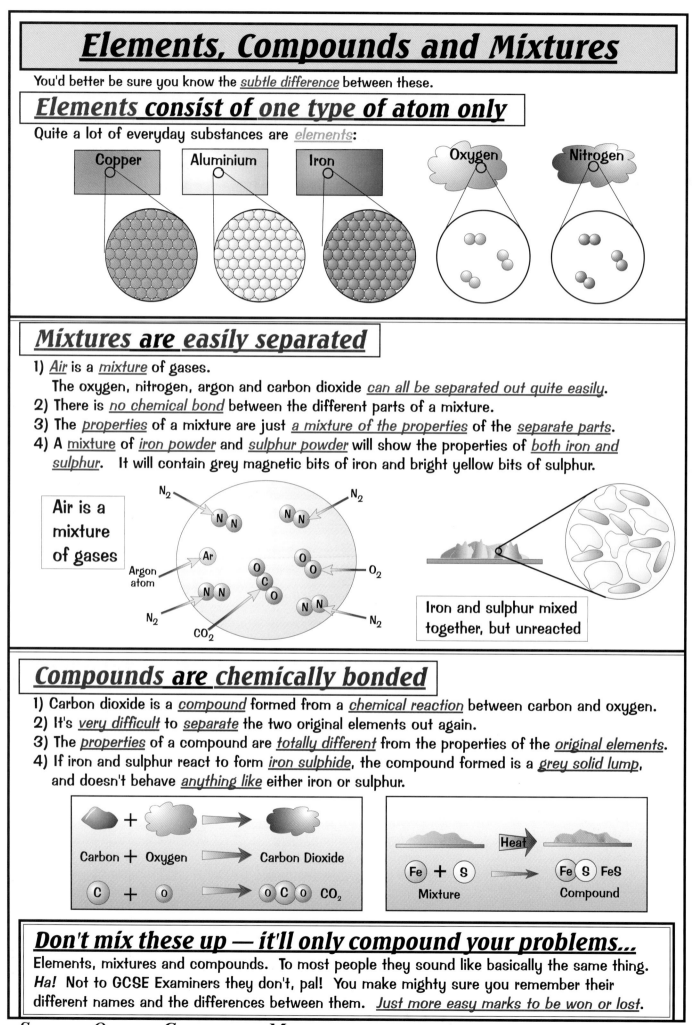

Copper   Aluminium   Iron   Oxygen   Nitrogen

Mixtures _are easily separated_

1) _Air_ is a _mixture_ of gases.
   The oxygen, nitrogen, argon and carbon dioxide _can all be separated out quite easily_.
2) There is _no chemical bond_ between the different parts of a mixture.
3) The _properties_ of a mixture are just _a mixture of the properties_ of the _separate parts_.
4) A _mixture_ of _iron powder_ and _sulphur powder_ will show the properties of _both iron and sulphur_. It will contain grey magnetic bits of iron and bright yellow bits of sulphur.

Air is a mixture of gases

N_2 N_2 Ar   Argon atom O_2 N_2 CO_2 N_2

Iron and sulphur mixed together, but unreacted

Compounds _are chemically bonded_

1) Carbon dioxide is a _compound_ formed from a _chemical reaction_ between carbon and oxygen.
2) It's _very difficult_ to _separate_ the two original elements out again.
3) The _properties_ of a compound are _totally different_ from the properties of the _original elements_.
4) If iron and sulphur react to form _iron sulphide_, the compound formed is a _grey solid lump_, and doesn't behave _anything like_ either iron or sulphur.

Carbon + Oxygen $\longrightarrow$ Carbon Dioxide

C + o $\longrightarrow$ o C o CO_2

Fe + S $\xrightarrow{\text{Heat}}$ Fe S FeS

Mixture   Compound

Don't mix these up — it'll only compound your problems...

Elements, mixtures and compounds. To most people they sound like basically the same thing. _Ha!_ Not to GCSE Examiners they don't, pal! You make mighty sure you remember their different names and the differences between them. _Just more easy marks to be won or lost._

13

Separation Techniques

There are _four separation techniques_ you need to be familiar with.

1) _FILTRATION_   2) _CRYSTALLISATION_   3) _CHROMATOGRAPHY_   4) _DISTILLATION_

The Separation of Rock Salt — salt and sand

1) They do like this for Exam Questions.
2) _Rock salt_ is a _MIXTURE_ of _sand_ and _salt_, so it's _easy_ to separate the salt from the sand.
3) Salt and sand are both _compounds_, so it'd be _difficult to split them_ into their _elements_.
4) _LEARN THE STEPS_ of this method for separating the mixture of sand and salt:

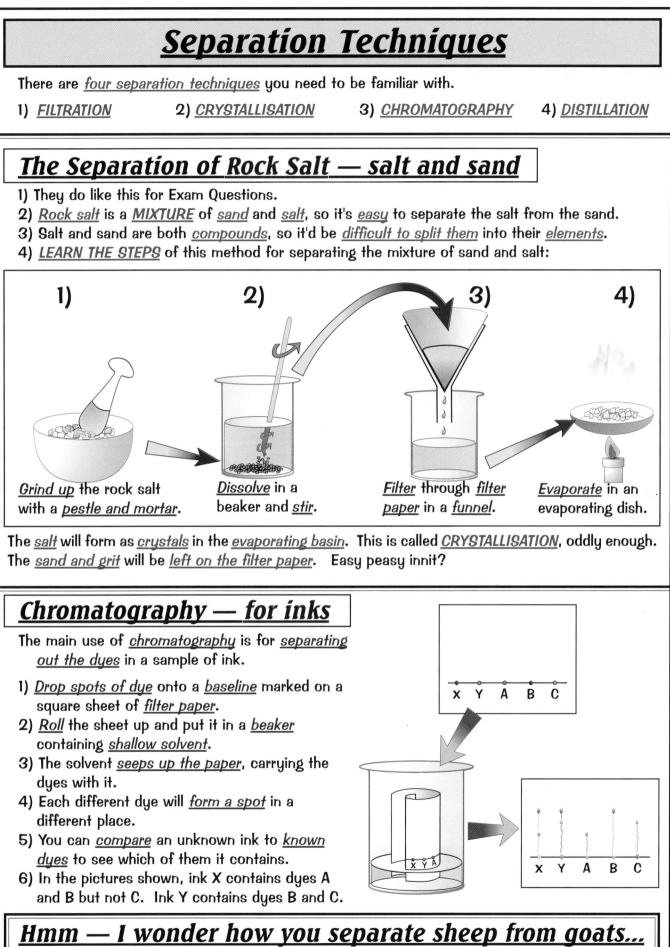

1) _Grind up_ the rock salt with a _pestle and mortar._

2) _Dissolve_ in a beaker and _stir_.

3) _Filter_ through _filter paper_ in a _funnel_.

4) _Evaporate_ in an evaporating dish.

The _salt_ will form as _crystals_ in the _evaporating basin_. This is called _CRYSTALLISATION_, oddly enough. The _sand and grit_ will be _left on the filter paper_. Easy peasy innit?

Chromatography — for inks

The main use of _chromatography_ is for _separating out the dyes_ in a sample of ink.

1) _Drop spots of dye_ onto a _baseline_ marked on a square sheet of _filter paper_.
2) _Roll_ the sheet up and put it in a _beaker_ containing _shallow solvent_.
3) The solvent _seeps up the paper_, carrying the dyes with it.
4) Each different dye will _form a spot_ in a different place.
5) You can _compare_ an unknown ink to _known dyes_ to see which of them it contains.
6) In the pictures shown, ink X contains dyes A and B but not C. Ink Y contains dyes B and C.

Hmm — I wonder how you separate sheep from goats...

Make sure you know all the details of separating the salt and grit from rock salt, because they really do like that for Exam questions. Chromatography is a big word but that's the only thing that's hard about it. Learn all this stuff. _Then cover the page and see what you know._

SECTION ONE — CLASSIFYING MATERIALS

Separation Techniques

Distillation — for obtaining pure water from all sorts

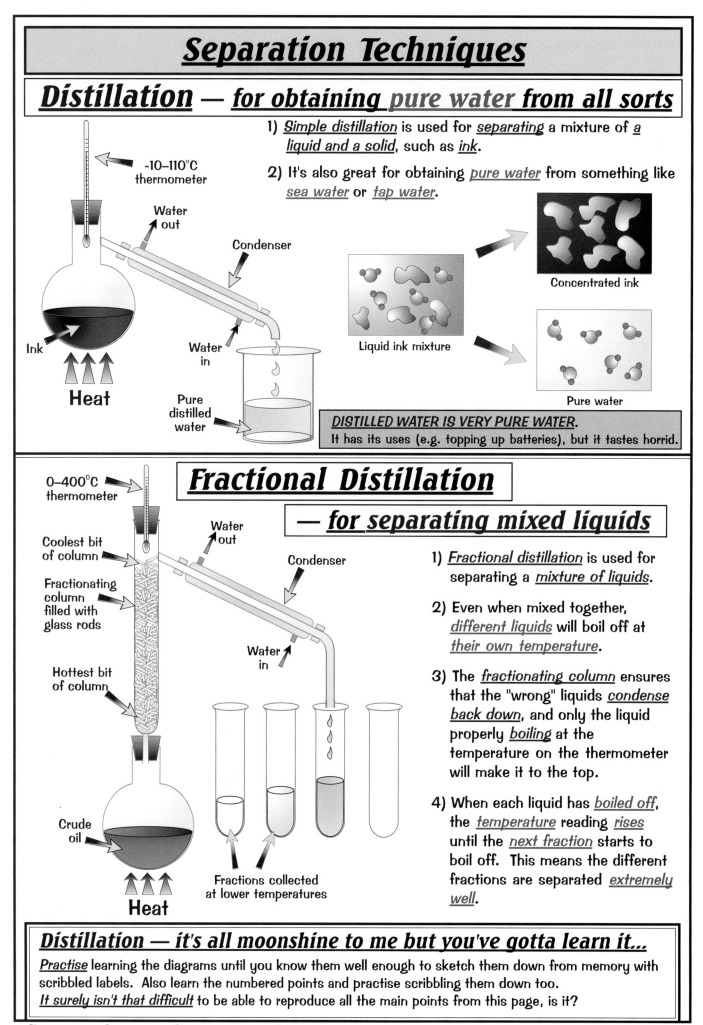

1) _Simple distillation_ is used for _separating_ a mixture of _a liquid and a solid_, such as _ink_.

2) It's also great for obtaining _pure water_ from something like _sea water_ or _tap water_.

-10–110°C thermometer

Water out

Condenser

Concentrated ink

Liquid ink mixture

Ink

Water in

Pure water

Heat

Pure distilled water

DISTILLED WATER IS VERY PURE WATER.
It has its uses (e.g. topping up batteries), but it tastes horrid.

Fractional Distillation
— for separating mixed liquids

0–400°C thermometer

Coolest bit of column

Fractionating column filled with glass rods

Water out

Condenser

Hottest bit of column

Water in

Crude oil

Fractions collected at lower temperatures

Heat

1) _Fractional distillation_ is used for separating a _mixture of liquids_.

2) Even when mixed together, _different liquids_ will boil off at _their own temperature_.

3) The _fractionating column_ ensures that the "wrong" liquids _condense back down_, and only the liquid properly _boiling_ at the temperature on the thermometer will make it to the top.

4) When each liquid has _boiled off_, the _temperature_ reading _rises_ until the _next fraction_ starts to boil off. This means the different fractions are separated _extremely well_.

Distillation — it's all moonshine to me but you've gotta learn it...

Practise learning the diagrams until you know them well enough to sketch them down from memory with scribbled labels. Also learn the numbered points and practise scribbling them down too.
It surely isn't that difficult to be able to reproduce all the main points from this page, is it?

Common Tests and Hazard Symbols

You need to know these *FIVE EASY LAB TESTS*:

1) Chlorine bleaches damp litmus paper

(i.e. it *turns it white*).

2) Oxygen relights a glowing splint

The standard test for *oxygen* is that *it relights a glowing splint*.

3) Carbon dioxide turns limewater milky

Carbon dioxide can be detected by its *turning limewater cloudy* when it's bubbled through it.

4) The three lab tests for Water

Water can be detected in three ways:
a) by its *boiling point of 100ºC*
b) by *turning white anhydrous copper sulphate* to *blue hydrated copper sulphate* (and getting hot)
c) by turning *anhydrous cobalt chloride paper* from *blue* to *pink*.

5) Lab test for Hydrogen — the notorious "Squeaky pop"

Just bring *a lighted splint* near the gas with air around.
If it's hydrogen it'll make a *"squeaky pop"* as it burns with the oxygen in the air to form H_2O.

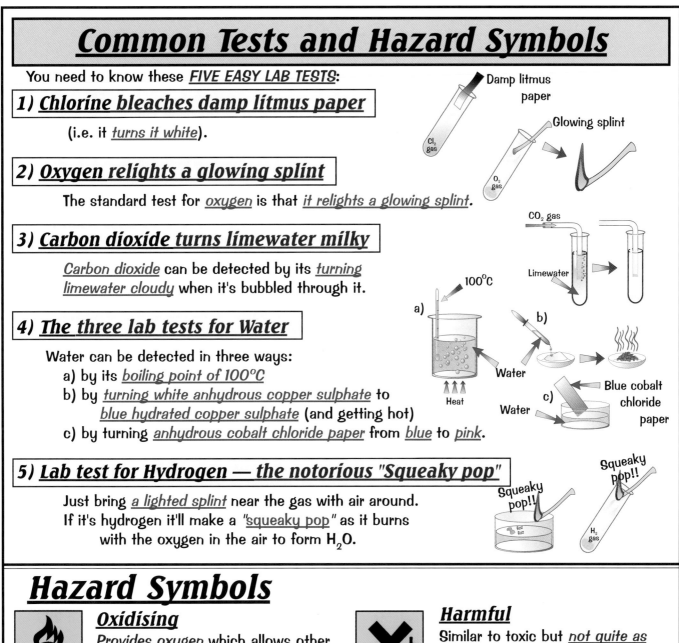

Hazard Symbols

Oxidising
Provides oxygen which allows other materials to *burn more fiercely*.
EXAMPLE: Liquid oxygen.

Highly Flammable
Catches fire easily.
EXAMPLE: Petrol.

Toxic
Can cause death either by swallowing, breathing in, or absorption through the skin. *EXAMPLE:* Cyanide.

Harmful
Similar to toxic but *not quite as dangerous*.
EXAMPLE: Petrol, meths.

Corrosive
Attacks and destroys living tissues, including eyes and skin.
EXAMPLE: Sulphuric acid.

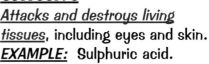

Irritant
Not corrosive but *can cause reddening or blistering of the skin*.
EXAMPLES: Bleach, children, etc.

Learn the Five Lab Tests — easy as squeaky pop...

This is pretty basic stuff, but people still lose marks in the Exam because they don't make sure to learn all the little details really thoroughly. That's true for just about everything in this book. It's no good just letting your eyes drift lazily across the page and thinking "Oh yeah, I know all that stuff". You've gotta really make sure you *do* know it all. *And there's only one way to do that* — so do it now.

Revision Summary for Section One

These certainly aren't the easiest questions you're going to come across. That's because they test what you know without giving you any clues. At first you might think they're impossibly difficult. Eventually you'll realise that they simply test whether you've learnt the stuff or not. If you're struggling to answer these then you need to do some serious learning.

1) What are the three states of matter?
2) Describe the bonding and atom spacing in all three states.
3) Describe the physical properties of each of these three states of matter.
4) What are the three ways of changing between the three states of matter?
5) Explain what goes on in all three processes, in terms of bonds and heat energy.
6) Sketch a heating graph and a cooling graph, with lots of labels.
7) Explain why these graphs have flat spots.
8) Sketch the equipment for observing Brownian Motion.
9) What do you see when observing Brownian Motion? Explain this behaviour.
10) Sketch three gripping diffusion experiments and explain what happens in them.
11) Sketch an atom. Give five details about the nucleus and five details about the electrons.
12) What are the three particles found in an atom?
13) Do a table showing their relative masses and charges.
14) How do the numbers of these particles compare to each other in a neutral atom?
15) What do the mass number and atomic number represent?
16) Explain what an isotope is. (!)   Give a well-known example.
17) List five facts (or "Rules") about electron shells.
18) What is ionic bonding? Which kind of atoms like to do ionic bonding?
19) Why do atoms want to form ionic bonds anyway?
20) What is covalent bonding?
21) Why do some atoms do covalent bonding instead of ionic bonding?
22) Give two examples of covalent molecules, and sketch diagrams, showing the electrons.
23) What kind of ions are formed by elements in Groups I, II, and those in Groups VI and VII?
24) Draw a diagram of a giant ionic lattice.
25) List the three main properties of ionic compounds.
26) What are the two types of covalent substances? Give three examples of each type.
27) Give three physical properties for each of the two types of covalent substance.
28) Explain how the bonding in each type of covalent substance causes its physical properties.
29) What is the difference between elements, mixtures and compounds?
30) Give three examples each of elements, mixtures and compounds.
31) What are the four different separation techniques?
32) Give an example of what you could use each one for.
33) Give details of the four stages in the separation of salt from rock salt.
34) Give details of how you could identify the dyes in a sample of ink.
35) What process would you use to obtain pure water from sea water?
36) Draw a diagram of the equipment you would use.
37) What process would you use to split crude oil into separate fractions?
38) Draw a diagram of the equipment you would use.
39) Give full details of the lab tests for these:
    a) Chlorine,   b) oxygen,   c) carbon dioxide,   d) water (3),   e) hydrogen.
40) Sketch the six Hazard Symbols, explain what they mean, and give an example for each.

SECTION ONE — CLASSIFYING MATERIALS

Crude Oil

Fossil Fuels were formed from dead plants and animals

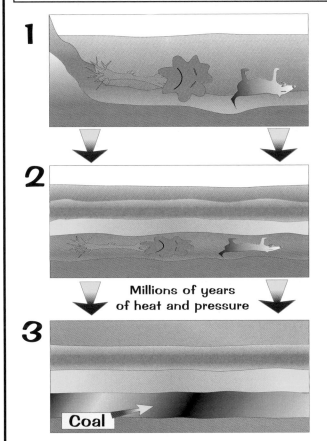

1) _Fossil fuels_ have formed over _millions of years_.

2) Plants and animals _died_ and were _immediately covered_ by _sediment_ in _seas_ or _swamps_.

3) This _stopped them decaying_.

4) _Further layers_ of sediment buried the plant and animal remains _deeper and deeper_.

5) After _millions of years_ of _pressure and heat_ (90°C to 120°C), these remains turned into _COAL_, _OIL_ and _NATURAL GAS_.

6) _Coal_ comes mainly from _dead plants_, like trees, falling into _swamps_.

7) _Oil and gas_ occur _together_ and were formed from _both plants and animals_ being buried.

8) Fossil fuels are made from the _"fossil" remains_ of plants and animals. Hence the name.

9) When we _burn_ fossil fuels we're using the _Sun's energy_ that has been _stored_ as _chemical energy_ underground for _millions_ of years.

Extracting Oil and Gas is pretty easy — once you find it

1) _Coal is solid_ so it just sits tight, waiting to be dug up.
2) _Oil and gas_ on the other hand tend to _move_.
3) They _seep upwards_ through _porous_ rocks such as sandstone, and _may_ reach the surface.
4) _If they do_ the gas _escapes_ and the oil forms pools of _black sludge_.
5) Once people realised how _useful_ the sludge was they started _drilling_ down for it.
6) Oil and gas can form into _large pockets_ if it gets _trapped_ under a layer of _non-porous_ rock.
7) Experts guess where there might be oil and they drill down.
8) When they strike lucky, the oil is _usually under pressure_ and comes up of its own accord.

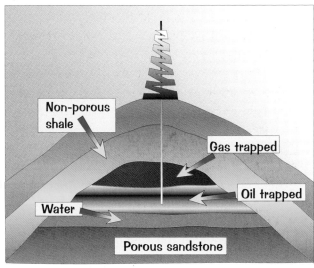

Revising for oil — you know the drill...

There are two sections on this page, with a total of 17 important points. You do realise they _won't_ ask you what colour oil is or whether it grows on trees or comes out of the ground, etc. No, they'll ask you about these more technical details, _so make sure you learn them all_.

18

Fractional Distillation of Crude Oil

1) *Crude oil* is a *mixture* of *hydrocarbons* of different sized molecules.
2) *Hydrocarbons* are basically *fuels* such as petrol and diesel.
3) The *bigger and longer* the molecules, the *less runny* the hydrocarbon (fuel) is.
4) *Fractional distillation* splits crude oil up into its separate *fractions*.
5) The *shorter the molecules*, the *lower the temperature* at which that fraction *condenses*.

Crude Oil is Split into Separate Hydrocarbons (fuels)

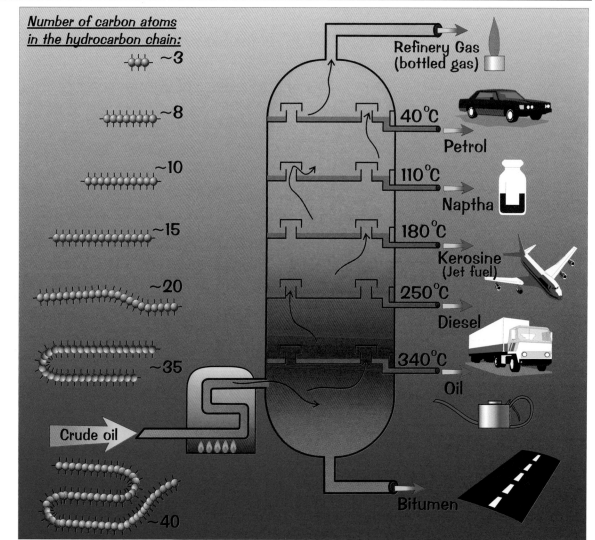

The *fractionating column* works *continuously*, with heated crude oil piped in *at the bottom* and the various *fractions* being *constantly tapped off* at the different levels where they *condense*.

Crude oil is a very big part of modern life

1) It provides the *fuel* for most modern transport.
2) It also provides the *raw material* for making various *chemicals* including *PLASTICS*.
   Plastics are just ace, of course. The world without plastics? Why, it would be the end of civilisation as we know it...

OK, so it's an easy page — don't let it go to your head...

A typical question would show a fractionating column and ask you which bit you'd expect petrol or diesel to come out of, or ask you how long the carbon chain of diesel is, or ask you to give the main uses of crude oil. So make sure you know *ALL* the details. When you think you do, *cover up the page* and *scribble down* all the details including the diagram. *Then try again.*

Using Hydrocarbons

Hydrocarbons are long chain molecules

As the *SIZE* of the *hydrocarbon molecule* *INCREASES*:

1) The *BOILING POINT* increases

2) It gets *LESS FLAMMABLE*
   (doesn't set fire so easy)

3) It gets *MORE VISCOUS*
   (doesn't flow so easy)

4) It gets *LESS VOLATILE*
   (i.e. doesn't evaporate so easily)

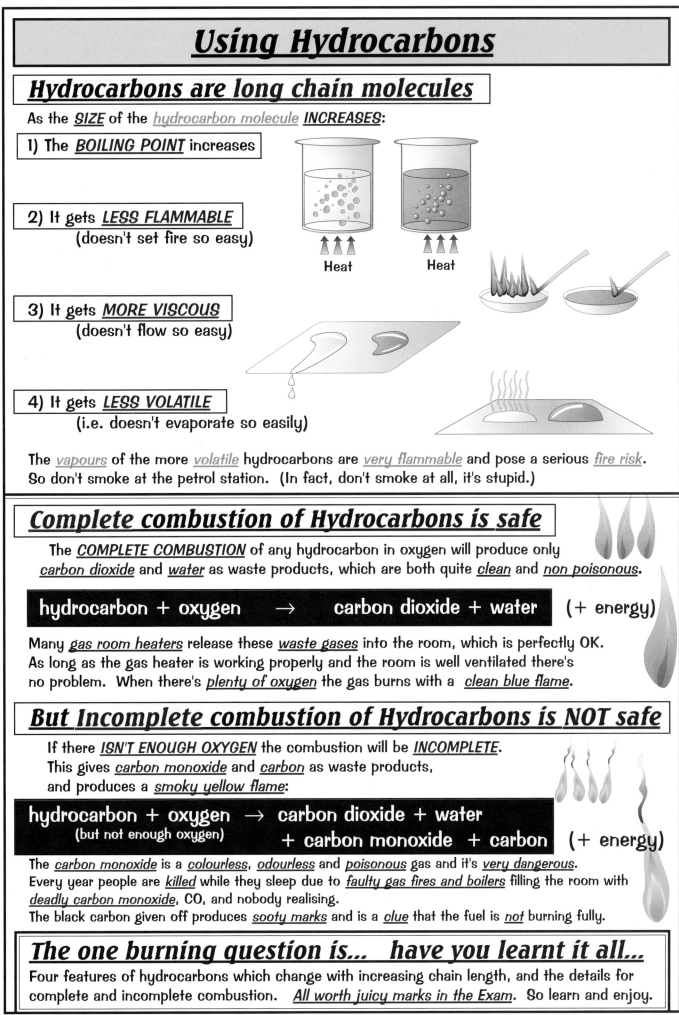

Heat   Heat

The *vapours* of the more *volatile* hydrocarbons are *very flammable* and pose a serious *fire risk*.
So don't smoke at the petrol station. (In fact, don't smoke at all, it's stupid.)

Complete combustion of Hydrocarbons is safe

The *COMPLETE COMBUSTION* of any hydrocarbon in oxygen will produce only
carbon dioxide and *water* as waste products, which are both quite *clean* and *non poisonous*.

$$\text{hydrocarbon} + \text{oxygen} \rightarrow \text{carbon dioxide} + \text{water} \quad (+ \text{energy})$$

Many *gas room heaters* release these *waste gases* into the room, which is perfectly OK.
As long as the gas heater is working properly and the room is well ventilated there's
no problem. When there's *plenty of oxygen* the gas burns with a *clean blue flame*.

But Incomplete combustion of Hydrocarbons is NOT safe

If there *ISN'T ENOUGH OXYGEN* the combustion will be *INCOMPLETE*.
This gives *carbon monoxide* and *carbon* as waste products,
and produces a *smoky yellow flame*:

$$\text{hydrocarbon} + \text{oxygen} \rightarrow \text{carbon dioxide} + \text{water}$$
(but not enough oxygen) $$+ \text{carbon monoxide} + \text{carbon} \quad (+ \text{energy})$$

The *carbon monoxide* is a *colourless*, *odourless* and *poisonous* gas and it's *very dangerous*.
Every year people are *killed* while they sleep due to *faulty gas fires and boilers* filling the room with
deadly carbon monoxide, CO, and nobody realising.
The black carbon given off produces *sooty marks* and is a *clue* that the fuel is *not* burning fully.

The one burning question is... have you learnt it all...

Four features of hydrocarbons which change with increasing chain length, and the details for
complete and incomplete combustion. *All worth juicy marks in the Exam*. So learn and enjoy.

Cracking Hydrocarbons

Cracking — splitting up long chain hydrocarbons

1) _LONG CHAIN_ hydrocarbons form _thick gloopy liquids_ like _tar_ which aren't all that useful.
2) The process called _cracking_ turns them into **SHORTER** molecules which are _much more useful._

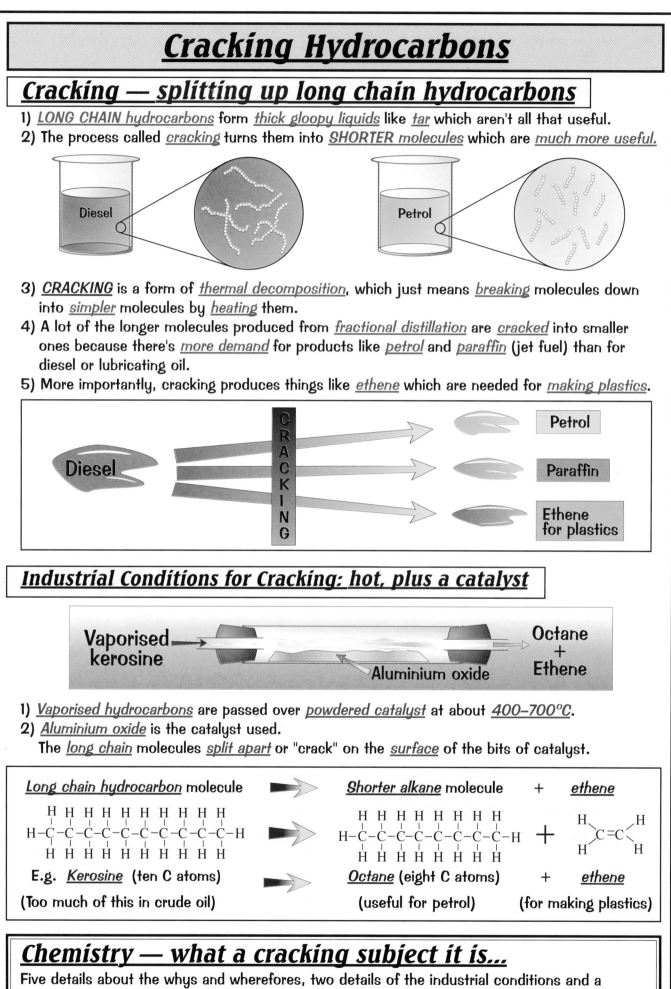

3) _CRACKING_ is a form of _thermal decomposition_, which just means _breaking_ molecules down into _simpler_ molecules by _heating_ them.
4) A lot of the longer molecules produced from _fractional distillation_ are _cracked_ into smaller ones because there's _more demand_ for products like _petrol_ and _paraffin_ (jet fuel) than for diesel or lubricating oil.
5) More importantly, cracking produces things like _ethene_ which are needed for _making plastics._

Diesel → CRACKING → Petrol / Paraffin / Ethene for plastics

Industrial Conditions for Cracking: hot, plus a catalyst

Vaporised kerosine → Aluminium oxide → Octane + Ethene

1) _Vaporised hydrocarbons_ are passed over _powdered catalyst_ at about _400–700°C_.
2) _Aluminium oxide_ is the catalyst used.
   The _long chain_ molecules _split apart_ or "crack" on the _surface_ of the bits of catalyst.

Long chain hydrocarbon molecule → _Shorter alkane_ molecule + _ethene_

E.g. _Kerosine_ (ten C atoms) → _Octane_ (eight C atoms) + _ethene_

(Too much of this in crude oil) → (useful for petrol) (for making plastics)

Chemistry — what a cracking subject it is...

Five details about the whys and wherefores, two details of the industrial conditions and a specific example showing typical products: a shorter chain alkane and ethene. _LEARN IT ALL._

Alkanes and Alkenes

CRUDE OIL contains *two different types* of hydrocarbons called *alkanes* and *alkenes*.
You don't need to know that much about them, except that *alkenes* have *C=C double bonds*.
You should know the first four *alkanes* as shown below, and also *ethene* as the easiest alkene.

ALKANES have all C–C SINGLE bonds

1) Alkanes are made up of *chains* of carbon atoms with *single covalent bonds* between them.
2) The first four alkanes are *methane*, *ethane*, *propane* and *butane*.
3) *Methane* is known as *natural gas* which comes out of the gas taps and is piped to our homes.
4) Alkanes *burn cleanly* producing *carbon dioxide* and *water*.

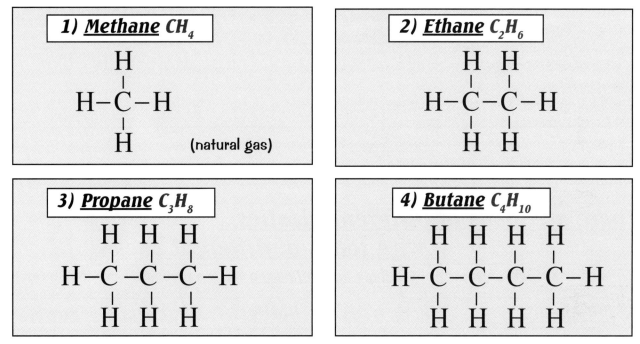

But ETHENE — well it has a C=C DOUBLE bond

1) The only *alkene* you need to know the name of is *ethene*, which is shown below.
2) Alkenes are *chains* of carbon atoms with some *double bonds* between the carbon atoms.
3) Alkenes will form *polymers* (see next page) by *opening up* their double bonds to "*hold hands*" in a long chain.
   Alkanes can't form polymers because they don't have any double bonds to open up.

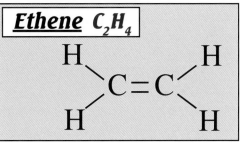

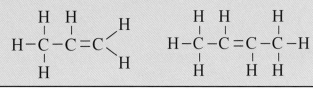

Here's two other alkenes and you can see the all important *double bond* in both of them.

Alkane anybody who doesn't learn this lot properly...

Four structural diagrams for alkanes and one for ethene, plus seven numbered points.
It really isn't that difficult to learn the whole page until you can scribble it down from memory.
Try doing it for five minutes: *Learn, cover, scribble, check, relearn, cover, scribble, check, etc.*

Polymers and Plastics

Polymers and plastics were first discovered in about 1933. By 1970 it was all too late. Those halcyon days when they made *proper* motor cars with leather seats and lovely wooden dashboards, were over. Sigh.

Ethene opens its double bonds to form Polymers

1) Under a bit of *pressure* and with a bit of a *catalyst* to help it along, ethene molecules will open up their *double bonds* and "join hands" to form *very long chains.*
2) These long chain molecules are called *polymers.*
3) Other alkenes will also do this but *ethene* becoming polyethene or "polythene" is the easiest example. Make sure you know about it:

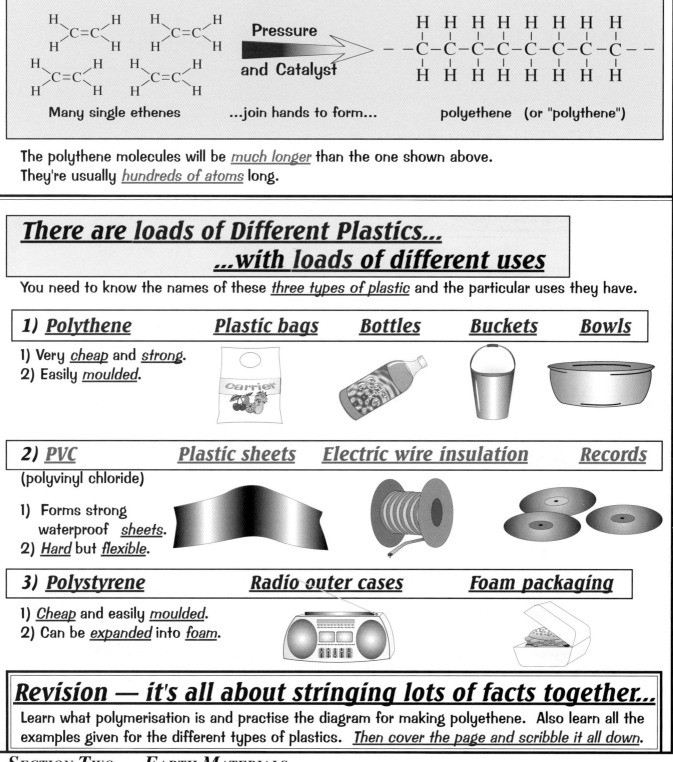

Many single ethenes   ...join hands to form...   polyethene (or "polythene")

The polythene molecules will be *much longer* than the one shown above.
They're usually *hundreds of atoms* long.

There are loads of Different Plastics...
...with loads of different uses

You need to know the names of these *three types of plastic* and the particular uses they have.

1) Polythene   Plastic bags   Bottles   Buckets   Bowls

1) Very *cheap* and *strong.*
2) Easily *moulded.*

2) PVC   Plastic sheets   Electric wire insulation   Records

(polyvinyl chloride)

1) Forms strong waterproof *sheets.*
2) *Hard* but *flexible.*

3) Polystyrene   Radio outer cases   Foam packaging

1) *Cheap* and easily *moulded.*
2) Can be *expanded* into *foam.*

Revision — it's all about stringing lots of facts together...

Learn what polymerisation is and practise the diagram for making polyethene. Also learn all the examples given for the different types of plastics. *Then cover the page and scribble it all down.*

Metal Ores From the Ground

Rocks, Minerals and Ores

1) A _rock_ is a mixture of _minerals_.
2) A _mineral_ is any _solid element or compound_ found naturally in the _Earth's crust_.
   Examples: Diamond (carbon), quartz (silicon dioxide), bauxite (Al_2O_3).
3) A _metal ore_ is defined as a _mineral_ or minerals which contain _enough metal_ in them to make it _worthwhile_ extracting the metal from it.

Metals are extracted from ores using Carbon or Electrolysis

1) _Extracting a metal_ from its ore involves a _chemical reaction_ to separate the metal out.
2) In many cases the metal is found as an _oxide_. There are three ores you need to know:

> a) _Iron ore_ is called _Haematite_, which is iron(III) oxide, formula Fe_2O_3.
> b) _Aluminium ore_ is called _Bauxite_, which is aluminium oxide, formula Al_2O_3.
> c) _Copper ore_ is called _Malachite_, which is copper(II) carbonate, formula $CuCO_3$.

3) The _TWO_ common ways of _extracting a metal_ from its ore are:
   a) Chemical _reduction_ using _carbon_ or _carbon monoxide_
   b) _Electrolysis_.

4) _Gold_ is one of the few metals found as a _metal_ rather than in a chemical compound (an ore).

More Reactive Metals are Harder to Get

1) The _more reactive_ metals took _longer_ to be discovered. (e.g. aluminium, sodium)
2) The _more reactive_ metals are also _harder to extract_ from their mineral ores.
3) The above _two facts_ are obviously _related_. It's _obvious_ when you think about it...

Primitive man could find gold easy enough just lying about in streams and then melt it into ingots and jewellery whilst watching Mrs Ug cook his mammoth-tail soup, but building a fully operational electrolysis plant to extract sodium metal from rock salt was unlikely to develop from his daily routine of hunting and cooking (well, being cooked for, anyway — cooking was woman's work after all — leaving the menfolk to get on with designing the electrolysis plant).

The Position of Carbon In the Reactivity Series decides it...

1) Metals _higher than carbon_ in the reactivity series have to be extracted using _electrolysis_.

2) Metals _below carbon_ in the reactivity series can be extracted by _reduction_ using _carbon_.

3) This is obviously because carbon _can only take the oxygen_ away from metals which are _less reactive_ than carbon _itself_ is.

The Reactivity Series	
Potassium	K
Sodium	Na
Calcium	Ca
Magnesium	Mg
Aluminium	Al
CARBON	C
Zinc	Zn
Iron	Fe
Tin	Sn
Lead	Pb

Extracted using _Electrolysis_

Extracted by _reduction_ using _carbon_

Miners — they always have to get their ore in...

This page has four sections with three or four important points in each.
They're all important enough to need learning (except the bit about the soup, etc.).
You need to practise _repeating_ the details _from memory_. That's the _only effective method_.

Extracting Iron — the Blast Furnace

Iron is a _very common element_ in the Earth's crust, but good iron ores are only found in _a few select places_ around the world, such as Australia, Canada and Millom.

Iron is extracted from _haematite_, Fe_2O_3, by _reduction_ (i.e. removal of oxygen) in a _blast furnace_.

You really do need to know all these details about what goes on in a blast furnace, _including the equations_.

The Raw Materials are Iron Ore, Coke and Limestone

1) The _iron ore_ contains the _iron_ — which is pretty important.

2) The _coke_ is almost _pure carbon_. This is for _reducing_ the _iron oxide_ to _iron metal_.

3) The _limestone_ takes away _impurities_ in the form of _slag_.

Reducing the Iron Ore to Iron:

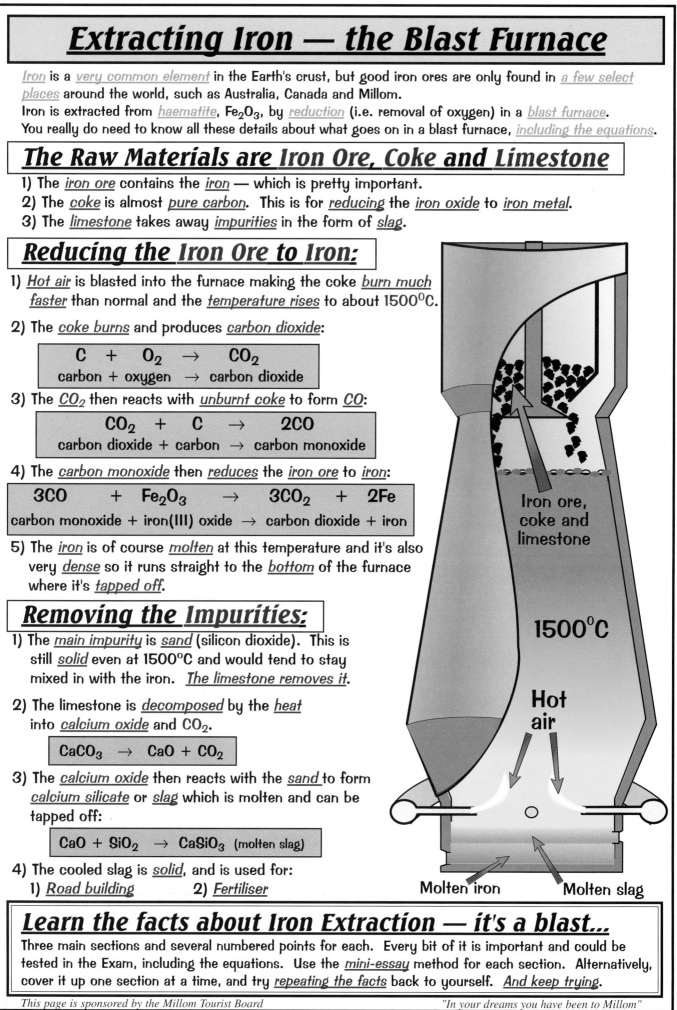

1) _Hot air_ is blasted into the furnace making the coke _burn much faster_ than normal and the _temperature rises_ to about 1500°C.

2) The _coke burns_ and produces _carbon dioxide_:

$$C + O_2 \rightarrow CO_2$$
carbon + oxygen → carbon dioxide

3) The _CO_2_ then reacts with _unburnt coke_ to form _CO_:

$$CO_2 + C \rightarrow 2CO$$
carbon dioxide + carbon → carbon monoxide

4) The _carbon monoxide_ then _reduces_ the _iron ore_ to _iron_:

$$3CO + Fe_2O_3 \rightarrow 3CO_2 + 2Fe$$
carbon monoxide + iron(III) oxide → carbon dioxide + iron

5) The _iron_ is of course _molten_ at this temperature and it's also very _dense_ so it runs straight to the _bottom_ of the furnace where it's _tapped off_.

Iron ore, coke and limestone

1500°C

Hot air

Removing the Impurities:

1) The _main impurity_ is _sand_ (silicon dioxide). This is still _solid_ even at 1500°C and would tend to stay mixed in with the iron. _The limestone removes it._

2) The limestone is _decomposed_ by the _heat_ into _calcium oxide_ and CO_2.

$$CaCO_3 \rightarrow CaO + CO_2$$

3) The _calcium oxide_ then reacts with the _sand_ to form _calcium silicate_ or _slag_ which is molten and can be tapped off:

$$CaO + SiO_2 \rightarrow CaSiO_3 \text{ (molten slag)}$$

4) The cooled slag is _solid_, and is used for:
   1) _Road building_   2) _Fertiliser_

Molten iron   Molten slag

Learn the facts about Iron Extraction — it's a blast...

Three main sections and several numbered points for each. Every bit of it is important and could be tested in the Exam, including the equations. Use the _mini-essay_ method for each section. Alternatively, cover it up one section at a time, and try _repeating the facts_ back to yourself. _And keep trying._

Purifying Copper by Electrolysis

1) Aluminium is a _very reactive metal_ and _has_ to be removed from its ore by _electrolysis_. (See P.26)
2) _Copper_ is a very _unreactive_ metal. Not only is it below carbon in the reactivity series, it's also below _hydrogen_, which means that copper doesn't even react with _water_.
3) So copper is obtained _very easily_ from its ore by _reduction_ with _carbon_.

Very pure copper is needed for electrical conductors

1) The copper produced by _reduction isn't pure enough_ for use in _electrical conductors_.
2) The _purer_ it is, the better it _conducts_. _Electrolysis_ is used to obtain _very pure copper_.

The _CATHODE_ starts as a _thin_ piece of _pure copper_ and more pure copper _adds_ to it.

Cathode (–ve)

Copper(II) sulphate solution containing $Cu^{2+}_{(aq)}$ ions.

Cu^{2+}

Anode (+ve)

The _ANODE_ is just a big lump of _impure copper_, which will _dissolve_.

Sludge

Pure copper is deposited on the pure cathode (–ve)

The reaction at the _CATHODE_ is:
$$Cu^{2+}_{(aq)} + 2e^- \rightarrow Cu_{(s)}$$

Copper dissolves from the impure anode (+ve)

The reaction at the _ANODE_ is:
$$Cu_{(s)} \rightarrow Cu^{2+}_{(aq)} + 2e^-$$

The _ELECTRICAL SUPPLY_ acts by:
1) _Pulling electrons off_ copper atoms at the _anode_ causing them to go into solution as _Cu^{2+} ions_.
2) Then _offering electrons_ at the _cathode_ to nearby _Cu^{2+} ions_ to turn them back into _copper atoms_.
3) The _impurities_ are dropped at the _anode_ as a _sludge_, whilst _pure copper atoms_ bond to the _cathode_.
4) The electrolysis can go on for _weeks_ and the cathode is often _twenty times bigger_ at the end of it.

Revision and Electrolysis — they can both go on for weeks...

This is a pretty easy page to learn. The mini-essay method will do you proud here. Don't forget the diagram and the equations. I know it's not much fun, but think how useful all this chemistry will be in your day-to-day life once you've learned it...
... hmmm, well... _learn it anyway_.

Extracting Aluminium — Electrolysis

There are quite a lot of technical details here which they quite like to test you on.
That means you gotta learn them, I'm afraid...

A Molten State is needed for Electrolysis

1) _Aluminium_ is _more reactive_ than _carbon_ so it has to be extracted from its ore by _electrolysis_.
2) The basic ore is _bauxite_, and after mining and purifying a _white powder_ is left.
3) This is _pure_ aluminium oxide, Al_2O_3, which has a _very high melting point_ of over 2000°C.
4) For _electrolysis_ to work a _molten state_ is required, and heating to 2000°C would be _expensive_.

Cryolite is used to lower the temperature (and costs)

1) Melting pure bauxite requires heating to 2000°C.
   This is expensive, so _instead_ the aluminium oxide is _dissolved_ in _molten cryolite_ (a less common ore of aluminium).
2) This brings the _temperature down_ to about 900°C, which makes it _much cheaper and easier_.
3) The _electrodes_ are made of _graphite_ (carbon).
4) The graphite _anode_ (+ve) does need _replacing_ quite often.
   It keeps _reacting_ with the oxygen to form CO_2.

The Cell Used in the Electrolysis of Aluminium Oxide

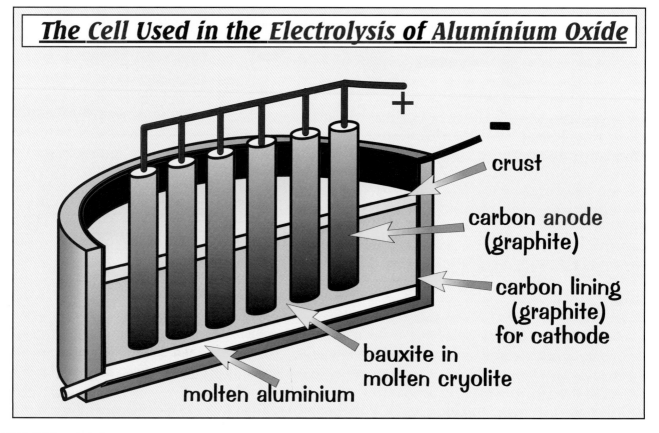

+

−

crust

carbon anode
(graphite)

carbon lining
(graphite)
for cathode

bauxite in
molten cryolite

molten aluminium

"Molten Cryolite" — a splendid name for a new town...

Learn the eight numbered points and the diagram. Initially you might find it easiest to cover the sections one at a time and try to _recall the details_ in your head.
Ultimately though you should _aim to repeat it all in one go_ with the whole page covered.

Extracting Aluminium — Electrolysis

You have to know how electrolysis does the business.
Have a real good look at this diagram and see if you can get the gist of it.

Electrolysis — turning IONS into the ATOMS you want

This is the _main object of the exercise_:
1) Make the aluminium oxide _molten_ to _release_ the aluminium _ions_, Al^{3+} so they're _free to move_.
2) Stick _electrodes_ in — so that the _positive Al^{3+} ions_ will head straight for the _negative electrode_.
3) At the negative electrode they just can't help picking up some of the _spare electrons_ and "_zup_", they turn into aluminium _atoms_ and they _sink to the bottom_. Pretty clever, I think.

Details of The Electrolysis of Aluminium Oxide

You need to know the _reactions_ at both electrodes:

At the Cathode (–ve):
$$Al^{3+} + 3e^- \rightarrow Al$$

At the Anode (+ve):
$$2O^{2-} \rightarrow O_2 + 4e^-$$

-ve Cathode (graphite)

O_2 and CO_2

+ve Anode (graphite)

Al^{3+} O^{2-}

'ZUP!' Al

Molten Cryolite

Molten Aluminium Metal

Electrolysis is Expensive — it's all that electricity...

1) Electrolysis uses _a lot of electricity_ and that can make it pretty _expensive_.
2) Aluminium smelters usually have _their own_ hydro-electric power station _nearby_ to make the electricity as _cheap_ as possible.
3) Energy is also needed to _heat_ the electrolyte mixture to 900°C. This is expensive too.
4) The _disappearing anodes_ need frequent _replacement_. That costs money as well.
5) But in the end, aluminium now comes out as a _reasonably cheap_ and _widely-used_ metal. _A hundred years ago_ it was a very _rare_ metal, simply because it was so _hard to extract_.

Electrolysis aint cheap — well, there's always a charge...

Learn the diagram showing how the electrolysis manages to extract aluminium metal from the molten mixture. Also _learn_ the three numbered points which explain it, and then the five numbered points about why it's so expensive. Then _cover the page_ and _scribble it down_ again.

Uses of The Three Common Metals

Metals are a lot more interesting than most people ever realise.   (Classic chat-up line No. 71)

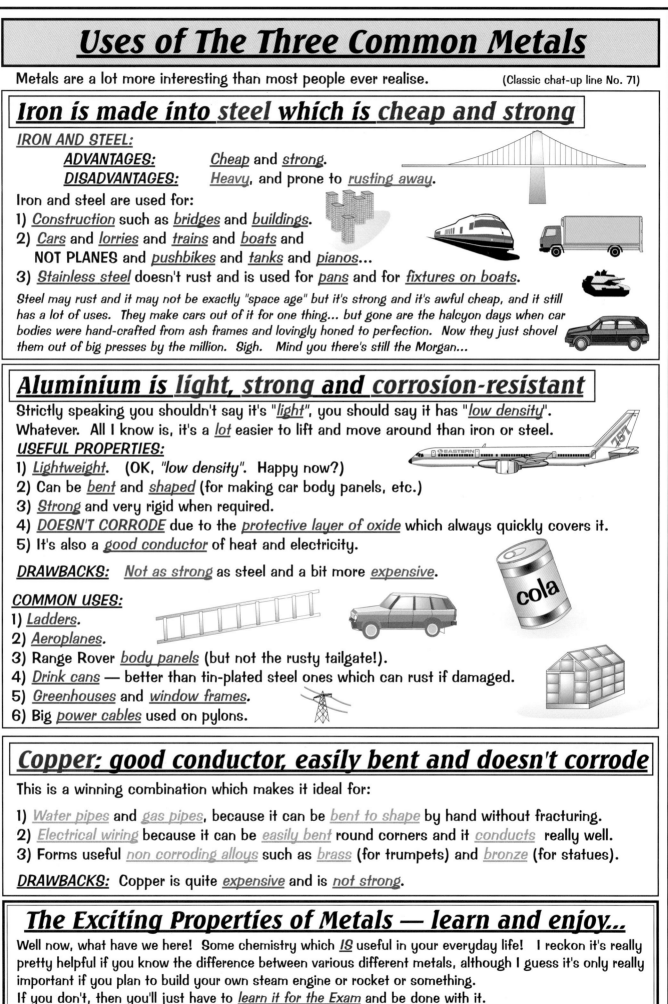

Iron is made into steel which is cheap and strong

IRON AND STEEL:
>   *ADVANTAGES:*   *Cheap* and *strong*.
>   *DISADVANTAGES:*   *Heavy*, and prone to *rusting away*.

Iron and steel are used for:
1) *Construction* such as *bridges* and *buildings*.
2) *Cars* and *lorries* and *trains* and *boats* and
    NOT PLANES and *pushbikes* and *tanks* and *pianos*...
3) *Stainless steel* doesn't rust and is used for *pans* and for *fixtures on boats*.

Steel may rust and it may not be exactly "space age" but it's strong and it's awful cheap, and it still has a lot of uses. They make cars out of it for one thing... but gone are the halcyon days when car bodies were hand-crafted from ash frames and lovingly honed to perfection. Now they just shovel them out of big presses by the million. Sigh.   Mind you there's still the Morgan...

Aluminium is light, strong and corrosion-resistant

Strictly speaking you shouldn't say it's "*light*", you should say it has "*low density*". Whatever. All I know is, it's a *lot* easier to lift and move around than iron or steel.

USEFUL PROPERTIES:
1) *Lightweight*.   (OK, "*low density*". Happy now?)
2) Can be *bent* and *shaped* (for making car body panels, etc.)
3) *Strong* and very rigid when required.
4) *DOESN'T CORRODE* due to the *protective layer of oxide* which always quickly covers it.
5) It's also a *good conductor* of heat and electricity.

DRAWBACKS: *Not as strong* as steel and a bit more *expensive*.

COMMON USES:
1) *Ladders*.
2) *Aeroplanes*.
3) Range Rover *body panels* (but not the rusty tailgate!).
4) *Drink cans* — better than tin-plated steel ones which can rust if damaged.
5) *Greenhouses* and *window frames*.
6) Big *power cables* used on pylons.

Copper: good conductor, easily bent and doesn't corrode

This is a winning combination which makes it ideal for:

1) *Water pipes* and *gas pipes*, because it can be *bent to shape* by hand without fracturing.
2) *Electrical wiring* because it can be *easily bent* round corners and it *conducts* really well.
3) Forms useful *non corroding alloys* such as *brass* (for trumpets) and *bronze* (for statues).

DRAWBACKS: Copper is quite *expensive* and is *not strong*.

The Exciting Properties of Metals — learn and enjoy...

Well now, what have we here! Some chemistry which *IS* useful in your everyday life! I reckon it's really pretty helpful if you know the difference between various different metals, although I guess it's only really important if you plan to build your own steam engine or rocket or something.
If you don't, then you'll just have to *learn it for the Exam* and be done with it.

Four Uses Of Limestone

Limestone is a _sedimentary rock_, formed mainly from _sea shells_. It is mostly _calcium carbonate_.

1) Limestone Used as a Building Material

1) It's great for making into _blocks_ for building with.
   Fine old buildings like _cathedrals_ are often made purely
   from limestone blocks. _Acid rain_ can be a _problem_ though.
2) For _statues_ and fancy carved bits on nice buildings.
   But _acid rain_ is even _more_ of a problem.
3) It can just be _crushed up_ into chippings and used for _road surfacing_.

2) Limestone for Neutralising Acid in lakes and soil

1) Ordinary limestone _ground into powder_ can be used to _neutralise acidity_ in lakes
   caused by _acid rain_. It can also be used to neutralise _acid soils_ in fields.
2) It works _better_ and _faster_ if it's turned into _slaked lime_ first:

Turning Limestone into Slaked Lime: first heat it up, then add water

1) The _limestone_, which is mostly _calcium carbonate_, is _heated_ and it turns into _calcium oxide (CaO)_:

| limestone $\xrightarrow{\text{HEAT}}$ quicklime | or | $CaCO_3 \xrightarrow{\text{HEAT}} CaO$ $+CO_2$ |

2) _Calcium oxide_ reacts _violently_ with _water_ to produce _calcium hydroxide_ (or slaked lime):

| quicklime + water $\longrightarrow$ slaked lime | or | $CaO + H_2O \longrightarrow Ca(OH)_2$ |

3) _Slaked lime_ is a _white powder_ and can be applied to fields just like powdered limestone.
4) The _advantage_ is that slaked lime acts much _faster_ at reducing the acidity.

3) Limestone and Clay are Heated to Make Cement

1) _Clay_ contains _aluminium_ and _silicates_ and is dug out of the ground.
2) _Powdered clay_ and _powdered limestone_ are _roasted_ in a rotating _kiln_ to produce
   a complex mixture of calcium and aluminium silicates, called _cement_.
3) When _cement_ is mixed with _water_ a _slow chemical reaction_ takes place.
4) This causes the cement to gradually _set hard_.
5) Cement is usually mixed with _sand and chippings_ to make _concrete_.
6) _Concrete_ is a _very quick and cheap_ way of constructing buildings — _and it shows_...
   — concrete has got to be the most hideously unattractive building material ever known.

4) Glass is made by melting Limestone, Sand and Soda

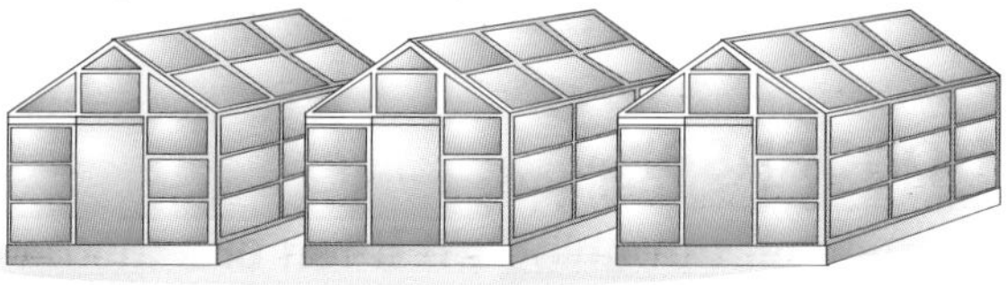

1) Just heat up _limestone_ (calcium carbonate) with _sand_ (silicon dioxide)
   and _soda_ (sodium carbonate) until it _melts_.
2) When the mixture cools it comes out as _glass_.
   It's as easy as that.
   Eat your heart out Mr Pilkington.

Tough Revision here — this stuff's rock hard...

I bet when those little sea creatures died all those millions of years ago, they had no idea they
would one day become the cornerstones of 20th century civilisation. Get it! — _cornerstones_.
Chortle chortle. Anyway, enough frivolity. _Learn the whole page_ till you've got it _rock solid_...

Revision Summary for Section Two

Section Two is pretty interesting stuff I reckon. Relatively speaking. Anyway, whether it is or it isn't, the only thing that really matters is whether you've learnt it all or not. These questions aren't exactly friendly, but they're a seriously serious way of finding out what you don't know. And don't forget, that's what revision is all about — finding out what you don't know and then learning it till you do. Practise these questions as often as necessary — not just once. Your ultimate aim is to be able to answer all of them easily.

1) What are fossil fuels? Why are they called fossil fuels?
2) Describe how fossil fuels formed. What length of time did it take?
3) Give details of how all three types of fossil fuels are extracted.
4) What does crude oil consist of?
5) Draw the full diagram of fractional distillation of crude oil.
6) What are the seven main fractions obtained from crude oil, and what are they used for?
7) What are hydrocarbons? Describe four properties and how they vary with the molecule size.
8) Give the equations for complete and incomplete combustion of hydrocarbons.
9) Which type is dangerous and why? What are the flames for these two types of combustion?
10) What is "cracking"? Why is it done?
11) Give a typical example of a substance which is cracked and the products that you get.
12) What are the industrial conditions used for cracking?
13) What are alkanes and alkenes? What is the basic difference between them?
14) Draw the structures of the first four alkanes and give their names.
15) Draw the structure of ethene and point out the important feature.
16) What are polymers? What kind of substances can form polymers?
17) Draw diagrams to show how ethene forms the polymer polyethene.
18) Name three types of plastic, give their physical properties and say what they're used for.
19) What are rocks, ores and minerals? Which metal is found as a metal rather than an ore?
20) What are the two methods for extracting metals from their ores?
21) What decides which method is needed?
22) Draw a diagram of a blast furnace. What are the three raw materials used in it?
23) Write down the equations for how iron is obtained from its ore in the blast furnace.
24) What is slag? Write two equations for the formation of slag, and give two uses of it.
25) How is copper extracted from its ore? How is it then purified, and why does it need to be?
26) Draw a diagram for the purifying process and give the two equations.
27) Describe how the pure copper is obtained.
28) How is aluminium extracted from its ore? Give four operational details and draw a diagram.
29) Explain how aluminium metal is obtained from the process, and give the two equations.
30) Explain three reasons why this process is so expensive.
31) Describe the plus and minus points of iron (and steel), and give six uses for it.
32) Describe the plus and minus points of aluminium, and give six uses for it.
33) Describe the plus and minus points of copper, and give three uses for it.
34) What are the four main uses of limestone?
35) Give the equations for turning limestone into slaked lime. Why do we bother?
36) Give four details about what cement is made of and how it works.
37) What is the Haber process? What are the raw materials for it and where are they obtained?
38) Draw a full diagram for the Haber process and state the temperature and pressure used.
39) Give full details of how ammonia is turned into nitric acid, including equations.
40) What is the main use of ammonia? Give the equation for producing ammonium nitrate.
41) Give two problems resulting from nitrate fertilisers. Explain fully what "eutrophication" is.

Nine Types of Chemical Change

There are _nine_ types of chemical change you should know about. It's well worth learning exactly what each of them is, _here and now_, rather than living the rest of your life in a confused haze.

1) THERMAL DECOMPOSITION — _breakdown on heating_

This is when a substance _breaks down_ into simpler substances _when heated_, often with the help of a _catalyst_. It's different from a reaction because there's only _one substance_ to start with. _Cracking of hydrocarbons_ is a good example of thermal decomposition.

2) NEUTRALISATION — _acid + alkali gives salt + water_

This is simply when an _acid_ reacts with an _alkali_ (or base) to form a _neutral_ product, which is neither acid nor alkali (usually a _salt_ solution).

3) DISPLACEMENT — _one metal kicking another one out_

This is a reaction where a _more reactive_ element reacts with a compound and _pushes out_ a _less reactive_ "rival" element. _Metals_ are the most common example. Magnesium will react with iron sulphate to push the iron out and form magnesium sulphate.

4) PRECIPITATION — _solid forms in solution_

This is a reaction where _two solutions react_ and a _solid_ forms in the solution and _sinks_. The solid is said to _"PRECIPITATE OUT"_ and, confusingly, the solid is also called _"a precipitate"_.

5) OXIDATION — _addition of oxygen_

Oxidation is the _addition of oxygen_. Iron becoming iron oxide is oxidation.

6) REDUCTION — _loss of oxygen_

Reduction is the _reverse of oxidation_, i.e. the _loss of oxygen_. Iron oxide is _reduced_ to iron.

7) EXOTHERMIC REACTIONS — _give out heat_

Exothermic reactions _give out energy_, usually as heat. "Exo-" as in "Exit", or "out". Any time a _fuel burns_ and _gives off heat_ it's an _exothermic_ reaction.

8) ENDOTHERMIC REACTIONS — _take in heat_

Endothermic reactions need heat _putting in_ constantly to make them work. Heat is needed to _form chemical bonds_. The _products_ of endothermic reactions are likely to be _more useful_ than the _reactants_, otherwise we _wouldn't bother putting all the energy in_, e.g. turning _iron oxide_ into _iron_ is an endothermic process. We need a lot of heat from the coke to keep it happening.

9) REVERSIBLE REACTIONS — _they go both ways_

Reversible reactions are ones that will cheerfully go in _both_ directions at the _same time_. In other words, the _products_ can easily turn back into the _original reactants_.

Nine more fantastic chat-up lines just waiting to happen...

A nice easy page to learn. You should know a lot of this already.
Anyway, cover the page and expose each yellow box (_without_ the other bit of the heading!) one by one and try to explain it to yourself before uncovering the text to check.

Balancing Equations

Equations need a lot of practice if you're going to get them right.
This is just a reminder of the basics.
But every time you do an equation you need to *practise getting it right* rather than skating over it.

The Symbol Equation shows the atoms on both sides:

Magnesium + Oxygen → Magnesium oxide
$2Mg$ + O_2 → $2MgO$

Balancing The Equation — match them up one by one

1) There must always be the *same* number of atoms on *both sides*, they can't just *disappear*.
2) You *balance* the equation by putting numbers **IN FRONT** of the formulae where needed.
   Take this equation for reacting sulphuric acid with sodium hydroxide:

$$H_2SO_4 + NaOH → Na_2SO_4 + H_2O$$

The *formulae* are all correct but the numbers of some atoms *don't match up* on both sides.
You *can't change formulae* like H_2SO_4 to H_2SO_5. You can only put numbers *in front of them*:

Method: Balance just ONE type of atom at a time

The more you practise, the quicker you get, but all you do is this:

1) Find an element that *doesn't balance* and *pencil in a number* to try and sort it out.
2) *See where it gets you.* It may create *another imbalance* but pencil in *another number* and see where that gets you.
3) Carry on chasing *unbalanced* elements and it'll *sort itself out* pretty quickly.

I'll show you. In the equation above you soon notice we're short of H atoms on the RHS.
1) The only thing you can do about that is make it $2H_2O$ instead of just H_2O:
$$H_2SO_4 + NaOH → Na_2SO_4 + 2H_2O$$
2) But that now causes too many H atoms and O atoms on the RHS, so to balance that up you could try putting $2NaOH$ on the LHS (Left Hand Side):
$$H_2SO_4 + 2NaOH → Na_2SO_4 + 2H_2O$$
3) And suddenly there it is! *Everything balances.* And you'll notice the Na just sorted itself out.

State Symbols tell you what Physical State it's in

These are easy enough, *just make sure you know them*, especially aq (aqueous).

(s) — Solid	(l) — Liquid	(g) — gas	(aq) — dissolved in water

E.g. $2Mg_{(s)}$ + $O_{2(g)}$ → $2MgO_{(s)}$

It's tricky — but don't get yourself in a state over it...

Balance these symbol equations, and put the rest of the state symbols in too:
1) $HCl_{(aq)} + Ca → CaCl_2 + H_2$ 2) $K_{(s)} + H_2O → KOH + H_2$
3) $HCl_{(aq)} + Na_2O → NaCl + H_2O$ 4) $CH_{4(g)} + O_2 → CO_2 + H_2O$

Electrolysis and The Half Equations

(Another psychedelic sixties pop group? Sigh... if only.)

Electrolysis means "Splitting Up with Electricity"

1) It requires a liquid, called the _electrolyte_ which will _conduct electricity_.
2) Electrolytes are usually _free ions dissolved in water_, e.g. _dilute acids_ like HCl, and _dissolved salts_, e.g. NaCl solution:
3) Electrolytes can also be _molten ionic substances_, but this involves _higher temperatures_. In either case it's the _free ions_ which _conduct_ the electricity and allow the whole thing to work.
4) The electrical supply acts like an _electron pump_, taking electrons _away from_ the _+ve anode_ and _onto the –ve cathode_. Ions _gain or lose_ electrons at the electrodes and _neutral atoms and molecules_ are released.

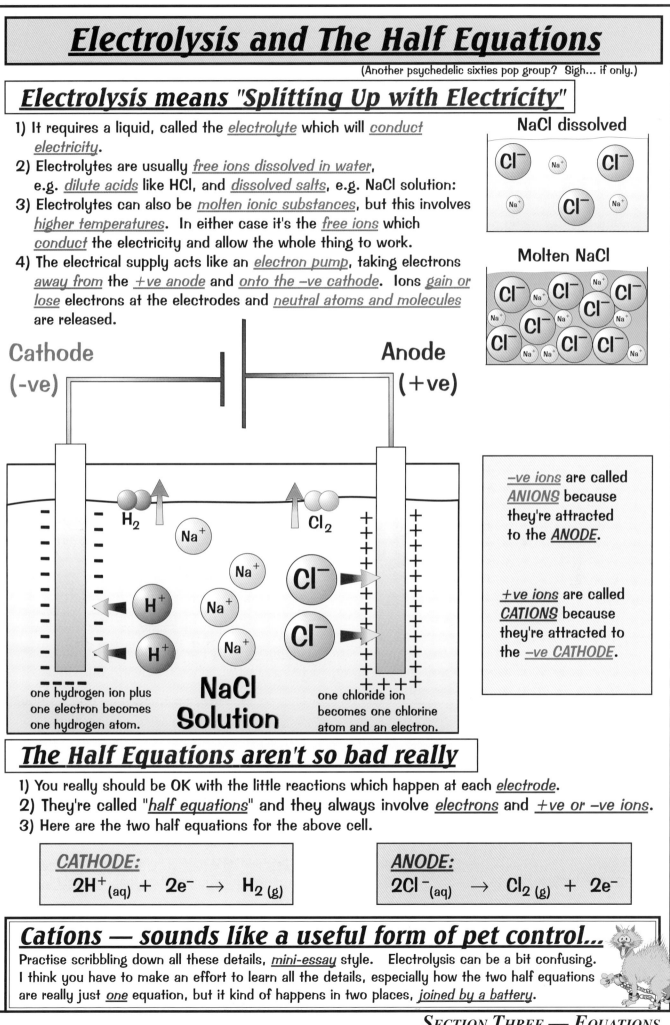

NaCl dissolved

Molten NaCl

Cathode (-ve)

Anode (+ve)

H₂

Cl₂

one hydrogen ion plus one electron becomes one hydrogen atom.

NaCl Solution

one chloride ion becomes one chlorine atom and an electron.

–ve ions are called **ANIONS** because they're attracted to the **ANODE**.

+ve ions are called **CATIONS** because they're attracted to the _–ve CATHODE_.

The Half Equations aren't so bad really

1) You really should be OK with the little reactions which happen at each _electrode_.
2) They're called "_half equations_" and they always involve _electrons_ and _+ve or –ve ions_.
3) Here are the two half equations for the above cell.

CATHODE:
$$2H^+_{(aq)} + 2e^- \rightarrow H_{2\,(g)}$$

ANODE:
$$2Cl^-_{(aq)} \rightarrow Cl_{2\,(g)} + 2e^-$$

Cations — sounds like a useful form of pet control...

Practise scribbling down all these details, _mini-essay_ style. Electrolysis can be a bit confusing. I think you have to make an effort to learn all the details, especially how the two half equations are really just _one_ equation, but it kind of happens in two places, _joined by a battery_.

Relative Formula Mass

The biggest trouble with *RELATIVE ATOMIC MASS* and *RELATIVE FORMULA MASS* is that they *sound* so bloodcurdling. *"With big scary names like that they must be really, really complicated."* I hear you cry. Nope, wrong. They're dead easy. Take a few deep breaths, and just enjoy, as the mists slowly clear...

Relative Atomic Mass, A_r — *easy peasy*

1) This is just a way of saying how *heavy* different atoms are *compared to each other*.
2) The *relative atomic mass* A_r is nothing more than the *mass number* of the element.
3) On the periodic table, the elements all have *two* numbers. The smaller one is the atomic number (how many protons it has).

   But the *bigger one* is the *mass number* (how many protons and neutrons it has) which, kind of obviously, is also the *Relative atomic mass*. Easy peasy, I'd say.

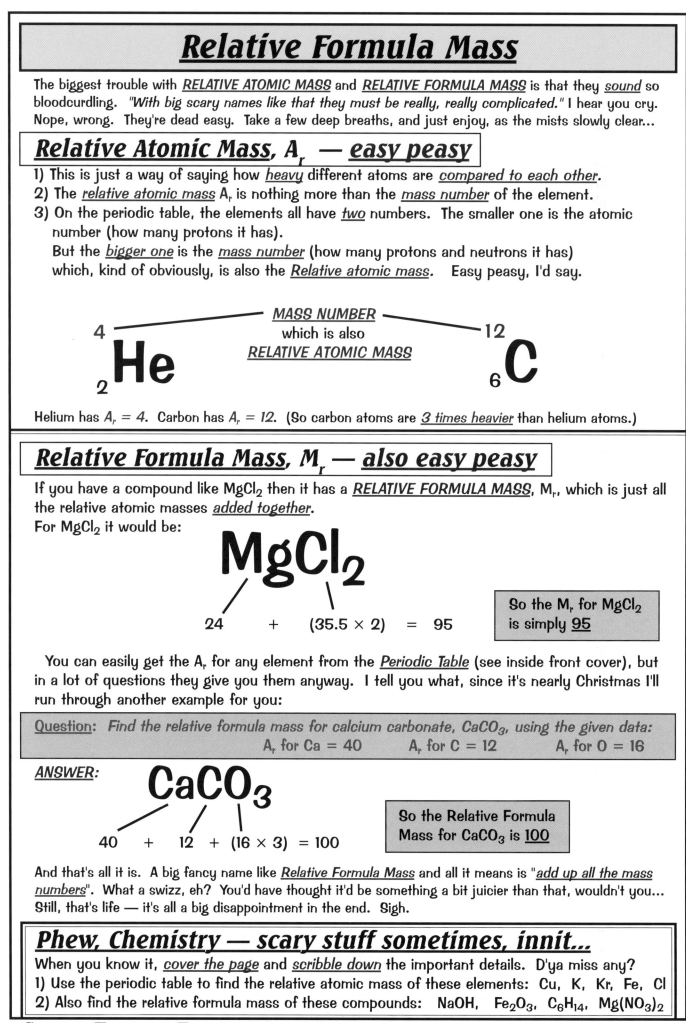

$$_2^4He \qquad \text{MASS NUMBER} \atop \text{which is also} \atop \text{RELATIVE ATOMIC MASS} \qquad _6^{12}C$$

Helium has $A_r = 4$. Carbon has $A_r = 12$. (So carbon atoms are *3 times heavier* than helium atoms.)

Relative Formula Mass, M_r — *also easy peasy*

If you have a compound like $MgCl_2$ then it has a *RELATIVE FORMULA MASS*, M_r, which is just all the relative atomic masses *added together*.
For $MgCl_2$ it would be:

$$MgCl_2$$
$$24 \quad + \quad (35.5 \times 2) \quad = \quad 95$$

So the M_r for $MgCl_2$ is simply **95**

You can easily get the A_r for any element from the *Periodic Table* (see inside front cover), but in a lot of questions they give you them anyway. I tell you what, since it's nearly Christmas I'll run through another example for you:

Question: *Find the relative formula mass for calcium carbonate, $CaCO_3$, using the given data:*
   A_r for Ca = 40 A_r for C = 12 A_r for O = 16

ANSWER:
$$CaCO_3$$
$$40 \quad + \quad 12 \quad + \quad (16 \times 3) = 100$$

So the Relative Formula Mass for $CaCO_3$ is **100**

And that's all it is. A big fancy name like *Relative Formula Mass* and all it means is "*add up all the mass numbers*". What a swizz, eh? You'd have thought it'd be something a bit juicier than that, wouldn't you... Still, that's life — it's all a big disappointment in the end. Sigh.

Phew, Chemistry — scary stuff sometimes, innit...

When you know it, *cover the page* and *scribble down* the important details. D'ya miss any?
1) Use the periodic table to find the relative atomic mass of these elements: Cu, K, Kr, Fe, Cl
2) Also find the relative formula mass of these compounds: NaOH, Fe_2O_3, C_6H_{14}, $Mg(NO_3)_2$

Calculating Percentage Mass

Although Relative Atomic Mass and Relative Formula Mass aren't too bad, it can get just a tadge *trickier* when you start getting into other calculations which use them.
The one you may well get asked in the Exam is calculating percentage mass...

Calculating % Mass of an Element in a Compound

This is actually dead easy — so long as you've learnt this formula:

PERCENTAGE MASS OF AN ELEMENT IN A COMPOUND $= \dfrac{A_r \times \text{No. OF ATOMS (of that element)}}{M_r \text{ OF WHOLE COMPOUND}} \times 100$

If you don't learn the formula then you'd better be pretty smart — or you'll struggle.
It's maybe easier to remember it in shorthand form like this:

$$\% \text{ MASS} = \frac{A_r \times n}{M_r} \times 100$$

EXAMPLE: Find the percentage mass of oxygen in potassium hydroxide, KOH
ANSWER:

1) As you know, the formula for finding % mass is: $\% \text{ MASS} = \dfrac{A_r \times n}{M_r} \times 100$
2) Using the periodic table we can work out values for A_r and M_r:
$\quad\quad\quad\quad A_r$ of oxygen $= 16$
$\quad\quad\quad\quad M_r$ of KOH $= 39+16+1 = 56$

3) Now we use the formula: $\underline{\% \text{ mass}} = \dfrac{A_r \times n}{M_r} \times 100 = \dfrac{16 \times 1}{56} \times 100 = \mathbf{28.6\%}$

And there it is. Oxygen is *28.6%* of the mass of potassium hydroxide, KOH.

EXAMPLE 2: Find the percentage mass of sodium in sodium carbonate, Na$_2$CO$_3$
ANSWER: *Follow these simple steps*

1) Once again, the formula for finding % mass is: $\% \text{ MASS} = \dfrac{A_r \times n}{M_r} \times 100$

2) Using the periodic table we can work out values for A_r and M_r:
$\quad\quad\quad\quad A_r$ of sodium $= \mathbf{23}$ (but watch out, 'cos there's *two* of them!)
$\quad\quad\quad\quad M_r$ of Na$_2$CO$_3 = (2 \times 23) + 12 + (3 \times 16) = 106$

$\quad$ Na$_2$ means 2 Na atoms, hence $23 \times 2 = 46$

3) Now we use the formula: $\underline{\% \text{ mass}} = \dfrac{A_r \times n}{M_r} \times 100 = \dfrac{23 \times 2}{106} \times 100 = \mathbf{43.4\%}$

And there you have it. Sodium (Na) is *43.4%* of the mass of sodium carbonate (Na$_2$CO$_3$).

Old Dmitri Mendeleev did this sort of stuff in his sleep — the old rogue...

Make sure you *learn the formula* at the top of the page. Then try these:
1) Find the percentage mass of oxygen in these: a) Fe$_2$O$_3$ b) H$_2$O   c) CaCO$_3$ d) H$_2$SO$_4$
2) Find the percentage mass of nitrogen in these: a) HNO$_3$ b) NO$_2$ c) KCN   d) Al(NO$_3$)$_3$

Revision Summary for Section Three

Some more horrid questions to stress you out. The thing is though, why bother doing easy questions? These meaty monsters find out what you really know, and worse, what you really don't. Yeah, I know, it's kinda scary, but if you want to get anywhere in life you've got to face up to a bit of hardship. That's just the way it is. Take a few deep breaths and then try these:

(Answers on P. 88)

1) What is meant by "thermal decomposition"?
2) Give an example of such a reaction.
3) What is neutralisation?
4) Give an example of a neutralisation reaction.
5) What is a displacement reaction?
6) Give an example of a displacement reaction.
7) What is a precipitation reaction?
8) Give an example of a precipitation reaction.
9) What is meant by an oxidation reaction?
10) Give an example of an oxidation reaction.
11) What is reduction?
12) Give an example of reduction.
13) What is an exothermic reaction?
14) Give two examples of exothermic reactions.
15) What is an endothermic reaction?
16) Give two examples of endothermic reactions.
17) What is meant by a reversible reaction?
18) Give two examples of reversible reactions.
19) Give three rules for balancing equations.
20) Balance these equations and put the state symbols in:
    a) $HCl + MgO \rightarrow MgCl_2 + H_2O$
    b) $HCl + Na \rightarrow NaCl + H_2$
    c) $CaCO_3 + HCl \rightarrow CaCl_2 + H_2O + CO_2$
    d) $Ca + H_2O \rightarrow Ca(OH)_2 + H_2$
    e) $Fe_2O_3 + H_2 \rightarrow Fe + H_2O$
    f) propane + oxygen $\rightarrow$ carbon dioxide + water

21) What is electrolysis? What is needed for electrolysis to take place?
22) Draw a diagram showing the electrolysis of NaCl solution. What are cations and anions?
23) What are the half equations for the electrolysis of NaCl solution?
24) What are A_r and M_r?
25) What is the relationship between A_r and the number of protons and neutrons in the atom?
26) Find A_r or M_r for these (use the periodic table inside the front cover):
    a) Ca   b) Ag   c) CO_2
    d) $MgCO_3$ e) Na_2CO_3 f) ZnO
    g) KOH   h) NH_3 i) butane
    j) sodium chloride   k) iron(III) chloride

27) What is the formula for calculating the percentage mass of an element in a compound?
    a) Calculate the percentage mass of oxygen in magnesium oxide, MgO
    b) Calculate the percentage mass of carbon in   i) $CaCO_3$ ii) CO_2 iii) methane
    c) Calculate the percentage mass of metal in these oxides: i) Na_2O ii) Fe_2O_3 iii) Al_2O_3

Today's Atmosphere

The atmosphere we have today is just right

1) It has *gradually evolved* over billions of years and *we* have evolved with it. All very slowly.
2) We worry that we're changing it *for the worse* by releasing various gases from *industrial activity*.
3) There are three main worries: *The Greenhouse Effect*, the *Ozone Layer* and *Acid Rain*. These are described in detail on P. 42 and P. 43.

Composition of Today's Atmosphere

The present composition of the atmosphere is:

> 78%   Nitrogen } (Often written as 79% Nitrogen for simplicity.)
> 1%   Argon
> 21%   Oxygen
> 0.04% Carbon dioxide
>
> Also :
> 1) Varying amounts of *WATER VAPOUR*.
> 2) And other *noble gases* in very small amounts.

(That comes to over 100% because the first three are rounded up very slightly)

Notice how very little carbon dioxide there is.

A Simple Experiment to find the % of Oxygen in the Air

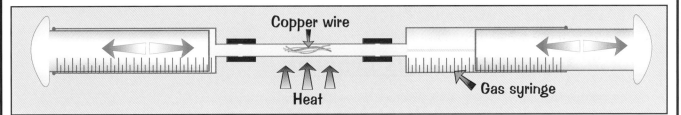

Method

1) Start with *one* gas syringe *pushed completely in*.
2) Take the reading off the full gas syringe to find the *initial volume* of air.
3) Then push it *back and forth* over the *heated copper*.
2) The copper *takes out* the oxygen and produces *black copper oxide*.
3) When *no more* copper is turning black, let it *cool* and measure the *amount* of air left.
4) As a *check* that all the oxygen has been *used up*, you then have to *heat* the copper *again* for a while and push the air back and forth over it again.
   Then you let it cool and *measure the volume again*.
5) Then you can *calculate* the percentage of oxygen in the air using this formula:

$$\text{Percentage of oxygen} = \frac{\text{Change in volume}}{\text{Original volume}} \times 100$$

Less than 1% water vapour? — so how come it's always raining...

This is all pretty simple. It's the kinda stuff that some of you might have thought doesn't need to be learnt. Tut tut tut tut tut tut. You should know better than that — d'ya really think I'd waste one of my precious pages on irrelevant junk? Nope. No way. *So learn it*.

The Evolution of the Atmosphere

The present composition of the atmosphere is:
78% Nitrogen, _21% oxygen_, _0.04% CO$_2$_ (= 99.04%)
The remaining 1% is made up of noble gases (mainly argon). In addition there can be a lot of water vapour.
But the atmosphere wasn't _always_ like this. Here's how the first 4.5 billion years have gone:

Phase 1 — Volcanoes gave out Steam, CO$_2$, NH$_3$ and CH$_4$

1) The Earth's surface was originally _molten_ for many millions of years. Any atmosphere _boiled away_.

2) Eventually it cooled and a _thin crust_ formed but _volcanoes_ kept erupting.

3) They _belched_ out mostly _carbon dioxide_.

4) But also some _steam_, _ammonia_ and _methane_.

5) The early atmosphere was _mostly CO$_2$_.

6) There was virtually _no oxygen_.
7) The water vapour _condensed_ to form the _oceans_.
8) _Holiday report_:
   Not a nice place to be. Take strong walking boots and a good coat.

Phase 2 — Green Plants Evolved and produced Oxygen

1) _Green plants_ evolved over most of the Earth.

2) They were quite happy in the _CO$_2$ atmosphere_.

3) A lot of the early _CO$_2$ dissolved_ into the oceans.

4) But the _green plants_ steadily _removed CO$_2$_ and _produced O$_2$_.

5) Much of the CO$_2$ from the air thus became _locked up_ in _the Oceans_ and also in _fossil fuels_ and _sedimentary rocks_.
6) _Holiday report_:
   A bit slimy underfoot. Take wellies and a lot of suncream.

The Evolution of the Atmosphere

Phase 3 — Ozone Layer allows Evolution of Complex Animals

1) The build-up of _oxygen_ in the atmosphere _killed off_ early organisms that couldn't tolerate it.

2) It also enabled the _evolution_ of more _complex_ organisms that _made use_ of the oxygen.

3) The oxygen also created the _ozone layer_ (O_3) which _blocked_ harmful rays from the Sun and _enabled_ even _more complex_ organisms to evolve.
4) There is virtually _no CO_2_ left now.
5) _Holiday report_:
   A nice place to be. Get there before the crowds ruin it.

The Oceans Now Hold a lot of Carbon dioxide

1) The _Oceans_ were formed by _condensation_ of the _steam_ in the early atmosphere.

2) They then started _absorbing_ the _CO_2_ from the atmosphere.

3) They now contain _a large amount of carbon dioxide dissolved_ in the water.

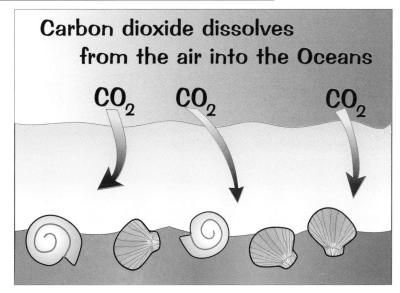

Coo... 4½ Billion Years — just takes your breath away...

I think it's pretty amazing how much the atmosphere has changed. It makes our present day obsession about the CO_2 going up from 0.03% to 0.04% seem a bit ridiculous, doesn't it! Anyway, never mind that, just _learn the three phases with all their details_. You don't have to draw the diagrams — but then it's a pretty good way to remember it all, don't you think. Yip.

Man-made Atmospheric Problems

Don't confuse these three different atmospheric problems. They're all *totally separate!*
(The Biology Book has more details on these. Well, it has more space for pretty pictures anyway.)

1) Acid Rain is caused by Sulphur Dioxide and Nitrogen Oxides

1) When *fossil fuels* are burned they release *mostly* CO_2 (which causes the Greenhouse Effect).
2) But they *also* release *two other* harmful gases, *sulphur dioxide* and various *nitrogen oxides*.
3) The *sulphur dioxide*, SO_2, comes from *sulphur impurities* in the *fossil fuels*.
4) However, the *nitrogen oxides* are created from a *reaction* between the nitrogen and oxygen *in the air*, caused by the *heat* of the burning.
5) When these gases *mix with clouds* they form dilute *sulphuric acid* and dilute *nitric acid*.
6) This then falls as *acid rain*.
7) *Cars* and *power stations* are the *main causes* of acid rain.

Acid Rain Kills Fish, Trees and Statues

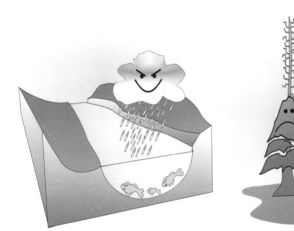

1) *Acid rain* causes *lakes* to become *acidic* and many plants and animals *die* as a result.
2) Acid rain *kills trees* and damages *limestone* buildings and *ruins stone statues*. It's shocking.

2) CFCs (from aerosols) Cause The Hole in The Ozone Layer

1) *Ozone* molecules are made of *three oxygen atoms*, O_3.
2) There's a *layer* of ozone *high up* in the atmosphere.
3) It *absorbs harmful UV rays* from the *Sun*.
4) *CFC gases react with ozone* molecules and *break them up*.
5) This *thinning* of the ozone layer allows *harmful UV rays* to *reach the surface* of the Earth.

Harmful UV rays

Ozone layer getting thin

CFCs rising up

City

6) But do remember, this has *nothing whatever* to do with the Greenhouse Effect or acid rain. Don't mix them up.

Man-made Atmospheric Problems

3) The Greenhouse Effect is caused by CO_2 trapping heat

1) The _Greenhouse Effect_ is causing the Earth to _warm up_ very slowly.
2) It's _caused mainly_ by a rise in the level of CO_2 in the atmosphere due to the _burning_ of massive amounts of _fossil fuels_ in the last _two hundred years_ or so.
3) The _carbon dioxide_ (and a few other gases) _trap the heat_ that reaches Earth from the Sun.
4) This will cause a _rise in temperature_ which is then likely to cause _changes in climate_ and weather patterns all over the world and _possible flooding_ due to the _polar ice caps melting_.

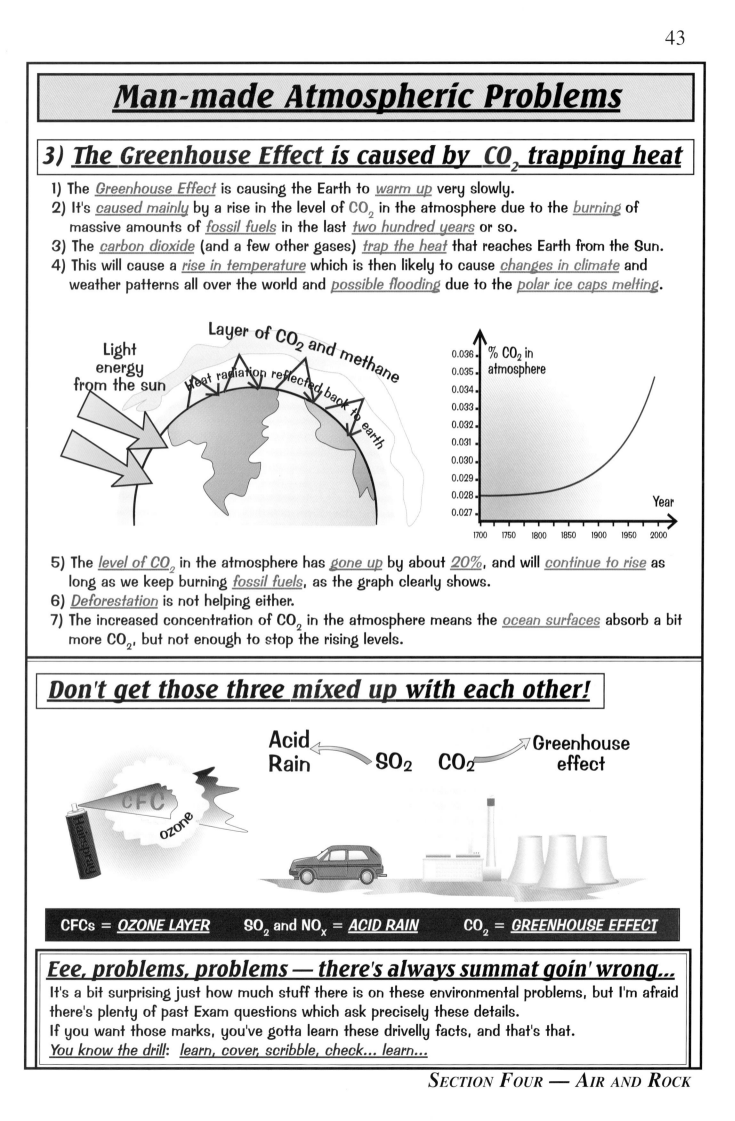

5) The _level of CO_2_ in the atmosphere has _gone up_ by about _20%_, and will _continue to rise_ as long as we keep burning _fossil fuels_, as the graph clearly shows.
6) _Deforestation_ is not helping either.
7) The increased concentration of CO_2 in the atmosphere means the _ocean surfaces_ absorb a bit more CO_2, but not enough to stop the rising levels.

Don't get those three mixed up with each other!

Acid Rain ← SO_2 CO_2 → Greenhouse effect

CFCs = _OZONE LAYER_ SO_2 and NO_x = _ACID RAIN_ CO_2 = _GREENHOUSE EFFECT_

Eee, problems, problems — there's always summat goin' wrong...

It's a bit surprising just how much stuff there is on these environmental problems, but I'm afraid there's plenty of past Exam questions which ask precisely these details.
If you want those marks, you've gotta learn these drivelly facts, and that's that.
You know the drill: _learn, cover, scribble, check... learn..._

The Carbon Cycle

The _Carbon Cycle_ shown below is a summary of how carbon passes through various forms and is constantly _recycled_. It's not as bad as it looks. Well, not once you _know it all_ anyway!

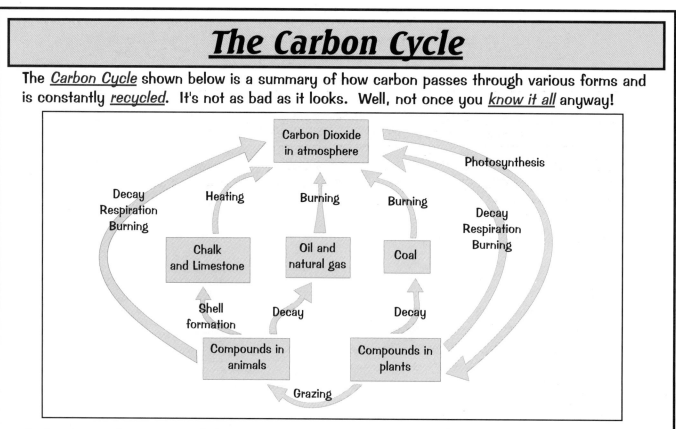

1) There's _another version_ of the carbon cycle given in the _Biology Book_ which is much better.
2) There are _many_ different ways of representing the carbon cycle, but in the end _they all show the same things happening_. If you _properly understand_ one diagram you should be able to deal with any other, even if it looks totally different. Apart from the pretty colours this is a _standard syllabus version_. That means it's like the one you'll probably get in your Exam.
3) This diagram just shows all the information, but _without_ trying to make it _clear_!
   Look at how this relates to the one in the Biology Book, which does try to make it clear.
4) This one also contains _chalk_ and _limestone_ which were left out of the biology one.
5) You should learn about all these processes elsewhere. This diagram is just a _summary_ of them.
6) In the Exam they could give you this diagram with _labels missing_ and you'd have to _explain_ or _describe_ the missing process, so it's _pretty important_ that you understand the _whole_ thing and know about each process.

7) The blank version here is for you to _practise_ on.

   Cover up the original and _fill it all in_ (_lightly_ with a pencil), bit by bit.

   Keep practising until you can do it. It's not as bad as it sounds. Really, it isn't.

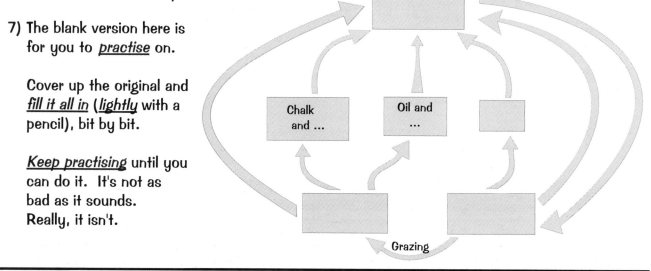

Learn and Enjoy...

The Carbon Cycle — one of the great highlights of the Double Science Syllabus, I'd say.

Weathering and the Water Cycle

(Sounds like an episode from "Last of The Summer Wine" — you can just picture the whole 30 minutes of it...)

Weathering is the process of breaking rocks up

There are _three_ distinct ways that rocks are _broken up_ into small _fragments_:

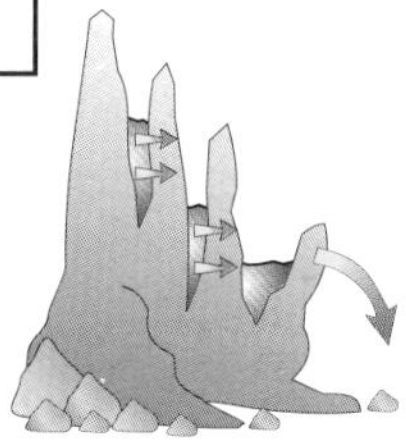

A) Physical weathering is caused by ice in cracks

1) _Rain water_ seeps into _cracks_ in rocks and if the temperature drops _below freezing_, the water turns to _ice_ and the _expansion_ pushes the rocks apart.
2) This keeps happening _each time_ the water _thaws and refreezes_.
3) Eventually bits of rock will _break off_.

B) Chemical Weathering is caused by acidic rain on limestone

1) This isn't just "acid rain" caused by pollution. _Ordinary rain_ is _weakly acidic_ anyway, so it very gradually _dissolves_ all _limestone_.

C) Biological weathering is caused by plant roots in cracks

1) _Plants_ push their _roots_ through cracks in rocks and as the roots _grow_ they gradually _push the rocks apart_.

Erosion and Transport

1) _Erosion_ is the _wearing away_ of exposed rocks, by any means. It's different from weathering.
2) _Transport_ is the process of _carrying away_ the rock fragments, either _falling away_ due to gravity, or being carried away _by rivers_. The rocks travelling down rivers get _worn down_ as they go and they also wear away the _river bed_ causing _river valleys_. The Grand Canyon is a grand example.

The Water Cycle

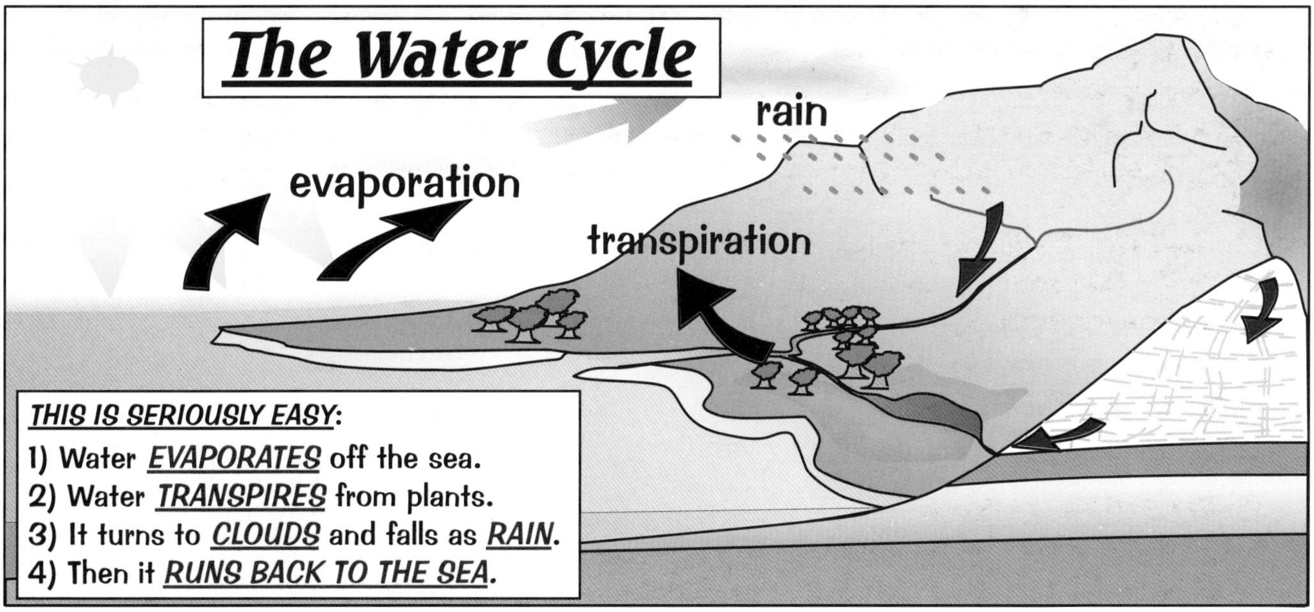

rain

evaporation

transpiration

THIS IS SERIOUSLY EASY:
1) Water _EVAPORATES_ off the sea.
2) Water _TRANSPIRES_ from plants.
3) It turns to _CLOUDS_ and falls as _RAIN_.
4) Then it _RUNS BACK TO THE SEA_.

FOUR EXTRA DETAILS: (which are only very slightly harder to remember than the diagram)

1) The _SUN_ causes the _evaporation_ of water from the sea.
2) _Clouds form_ because: when _air rises_, it _cools_, and the _water condenses_ out.
3) When the condensed droplets get _too big_ they _fall as rain_.
4) Some water is taken up by _roots_ and _evaporates from trees_ without ever reaching the _sea_.

Page after Page of sheer toil — it can wear you down...

Ooh, this is all really easy stuff isn't it. The only tricky bit is remembering the fancy words, like "erosion" and "chemical weathering", and exactly what they are. You know, "erosion" isn't quite the same as "weathering", for example. It's the same old method though: _Learn it, then cover the page, etc._

The Three Different Types of Rocks

Rocks shouldn't be confusing. There are _three_ different types: _sedimentary_, _metamorphic_ and _igneous_. Over _millions of years_ they _change from one into another_. This is called the _Rock Cycle_. Astonishingly.

The Rock Cycle

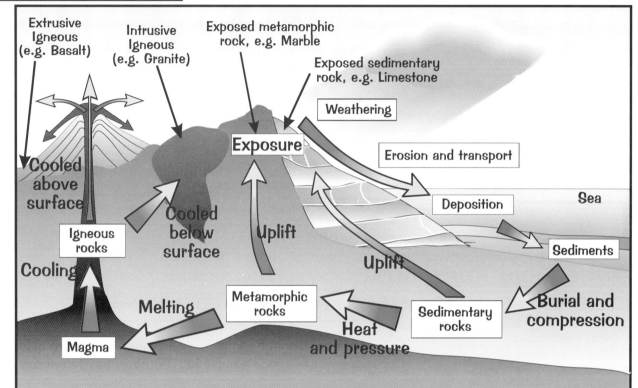

The Rocks Change from One to Another in a Slow Cycle

1) Particles get _washed to the sea_ and settle as _sediment_.
2) Over _millions of years_ these sediments get _crushed_ into **SEDIMENTARY** _rocks_ (hence the name).
3) At first they get _buried_, but they can either _rise to the surface_ again to be discovered, or they can _descend_ into the _heat_ and _pressure_ below.
4) If they _do_, the heat and pressure _completely alter_ the _structure_ of the rock and they then become **METAMORPHIC ROCKS** (as in "metamorphosis" or "change". Another good name!).
5) These _metamorphic rocks_ can either _rise to the surface_ to be discovered by an enthusiastic geologist or else descend _still further_ into the _fiery abyss_ of the Earth's raging inferno where they will _melt_ and become _magma_.
6) When _magma_ reaches the surface it _cools_ and _sets_ and is then called **IGNEOUS ROCK**.
   ("igneous" as in "ignite" or "fire" — another cool name. Gee, if only biology names were this sensible.)
7) There are actually _two types_ of igneous rock:
   1) **EXTRUSIVE** when it comes _straight out_ of the surface from a _volcano_ ("Ex-" as in "Exit").
   2) **INTRUSIVE** when it just sets as a big lump _below_ the surface ("In-" as in "Inside")
      (I have to say — whoever invented these names deserves a medal.)
8) When any of these rocks reach the _surface_, then _weathering_ begins and they gradually get _worn down_ and carried off _to the sea_ and the whole cycle _starts over again_... Simple, innit?

Rocks are a mystery — no, no, it's sedimentary my Dear Watson...

Don't you think the Rock Cycle is pretty ace? Can you think of anything you'd rather do than go on a family holiday to Cornwall, gazing at the cliffs and marvelling at the different types of rocks and stuff? Exactly. (And even if you can, it's still a good plan to _learn about rocks_.)

Sedimentary Rocks

Three steps in the Formation of Sedimentary Rocks

1) _Sedimentary rocks_ are formed from _layers of sediment_ laid down in _lakes_ or _seas_.
2) Over _millions of years_ the layers get _buried_ under more layers and the _weight_ pressing down _squeezes out_ the water.
3) As the water disappears, _salts crystallise out_ and _cement_ the particles together.

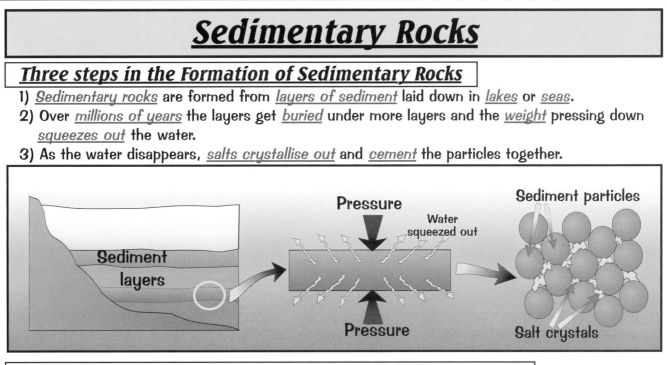

Fossils are only found in Sedimentary Rocks

1) Only _sedimentary_ rocks contain _fossils_. The _other two types_ of rock, metamorphic and igneous, have been through _too much heat and trauma_ to have fossils left in them.
2) Sedimentary rocks have only been _gently crushed_ for a few million years. _No big deal_, so the _fossils survive_. All sedimentary rocks are likely to contain fossils.
3) Fossils are a very useful way of _identifying rocks_ as being of the _same age_.
4) This is because fossilised remains that are found _change_ (due to evolution) as the _ages pass_.
5) This means that if two rocks have the _same fossils_ they must be from the _same age_.
6) However, if the fossils in two rocks are _different_, it proves _nothing_ don't forget!

The Four Main Sedimentary Rocks

Sedimentary rocks tend to _look similar_ to the _original sediments_ from which they formed. After all, _very little_ has happened other than them _squashing together_.

1) Sandstone

This is formed from _sand_ of course. And it looks like it too. Sandstone just looks like _sand particles_ all stuck _very firmly_ together. There's _red_ sandstone and _yellow_ sandstone which are commonly used for _buildings_. The now famous Barrow Town Hall is built in red sandstone.

2) Limestone

This formed from _seashells_. It's mostly _calcium carbonate_ and _grey/white_ in colour. The original _shells_ are mostly _crushed_ but there are still quite a few _fossilised shells_ to be found in _limestone_.

3) Mudstone or shale

This was formed from _mud_ which basically means _finer particles than sand_. It's often _dark grey_ and tends to _split_ into the _original layers_ very easily.

4) Conglomerates

These look like a sort of crude _concrete_, containing _pebbles_ set into a _cement_ of finer particles.

Revision Pressure — don't get crushed by it...

Quite a lot of facts here on sedimentary rocks. You've gotta _learn_ how they form, that they contain fossils, and also the names etc. of the four examples. Most important you need to be able to _describe_ in words _what they all look like_. Even if you don't really know, just learn the descriptions!

Metamorphic Rocks

Heat and Pressure over Thousands of Years

Metamorphic rocks are formed by the action of *heat and pressure* on existing (*sedimentary*) rocks over *long periods* of time.

1) *Earth movements* can push *all types* of rock *deep underground*.

2) Here they are *compressed* and *heated*, and the *mineral structure* and *texture* may change.

3) So long as they don't actually *melt* they are classed as *metamorphic* rocks.

4) *If they melt* and turn to *magma*, they're *gone*. The magma may resurface as igneous rocks.

Possible uplift to the surface

Pressure from rocks above

Metamorphic Rock forming here

Magma

Intense heat from below

Slate, Marble and Schist are Metamorphic Rocks

1) Slate is formed from mudstone or clay

1) As the *mudstone* gets *heated* and *compressed* its tiny *plate-like particles* align in the *same direction*.
2) This allows the resulting *slate* to be *split* along that direction into *thin sheets* which make *ideal roofing material*.
3) The increasingly famous Barrow Town Hall has a slate roof.

2) Marble is formed from Limestone

1) Very high temperature will *break down* the *shells* in limestone and they reform as *small crystals*.
2) This gives marble a *more even texture* and makes it *much harder*.
3) It can be *polished up* and often has *attractive patterning*.
4) This makes it a great *decorative stone*. My Uncle Cyril has a fabulous Marble Headstone.

3) Schist is Formed when Mudstone gets real hot

1) Mudstone will turn to slate only if there's plenty of pressure but *not* too much heat.
2) If mudstone gets *really hot*, *new minerals* like *mica* start to form and create *layers*.
3) This creates *Schist*, a rock containing *bands of interlocking crystals*.
4) These *layers of crystals* are typical of a *metamorphic* rock.
5) Only *steady heat and pressure* will cause this to happen.

Schist! — when the heat and pressure is all too much...

There's quite a lot of names accumulating now. Somehow, you've got to make sense of them in your head. It really does help *if you know what these rocks actually look like* in real life.
It's best if you can think of specific objects made of them. Otherwise, it'll all get pretty tricky.

SECTION FOUR — AIR AND ROCK

Igneous Rocks

Igneous Rocks are formed from Fresh Magma

1) *Igneous rocks* form when *molten magma* pushes up *into the crust* or *right through it*.

2) Igneous rocks contain *various different minerals* in *randomly*-arranged interlocking *crystals*.

3) There are *two types* of igneous rocks: *EXTRUSIVE* and *INTRUSIVE*:

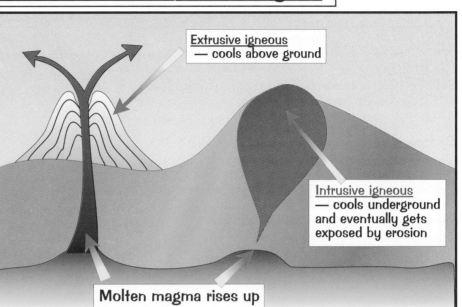

Extrusive igneous — cools above ground

Intrusive igneous — cools underground and eventually gets exposed by erosion

Molten magma rises up

INTRUSIVE igneous rocks cool SLOWLY with BIG crystals

GRANITE is an intrusive igneous rock with big crystals

1) *Granite* is formed *underground* where the magma *cools down slowly*.
2) This means it has *big* randomly-arranged *crystals* because it cools down *slowly*.
3) Granite is a *very hard* and *decorative* stone ideal for *steps* and *buildings*.
4) Barrow Town Hall? Don't know.

EXTRUSIVE igneous rocks cool QUICKLY with SMALL crystals

BASALT is an extrusive igneous rock with small crystals

1) *Basalt* is formed *on top* of the Earth's crust after *bursting out* of a *volcano*.
2) This means it has *relatively small* crystals — because it *cooled quickly*.

Identifying Rocks in Exam Questions

A typical question will simply *describe* a rock and ask you to *identify it*. Make sure you learn the information on rocks well enough to work *backwards*, as it were, so that you can *identify* the type of rock from a description. *Practise* by doing these:

Rock A: Small crystals in layers.
Rock B: Contains fossils.
Rock C: Randomly arranged crystals of various types.
Rock D: Hard, smooth and with wavy layers of crystals.
Rock E: Large crystals. Very hard wearing.
Rock F: Sandy texture. Fairly soft.

Answers
A: metamorphic
B: sedimentary
C: igneous
D: metamorphic
E: igneous (granite)
F: sedimentary (sandstone)

Igneous Rocks are real cool — or they're magma...

It's very important that you know what granite looks like. You really should insist that "Teach" organises a field trip to see the famous pink granite coast of Brittany. About two weeks should be enough time to fully appreciate it. In May. Failing that, sit and *learn this page* in cold grey England for ten minutes.

The Earth's Structure

Crust, Mantle, Outer and Inner Core

1) The _crust_ is very _thin_ (well, about 20km or so!).
2) The _mantle_ is _liquid_ but very _viscous_.
3) The _core_ is just over _half_ the Earth's radius.
4) The _core_ is made from _iron and nickel_. This is where the Earth's _magnetic field_ originates.
5) The iron and nickel _sank_ to the "bottom" long ago (i.e. the centre of the Earth) because they're _denser_.
6) The core has a _solid inner_ bit and a _liquid outer_ bit.
7) _Radioactive decay_ creates all the _heat_ inside the Earth.
8) This heat causes the _convection currents_ which cause the _plates_ of the crust to _move_.

crust

mantle

solid inner core of iron and nickel

liquid outer core of iron and nickel

Big Clues: Seismic Waves, Magnetism and Meteorites

1) The _overall density_ of the Earth is much _higher_ than the density of _rock_. This means the _inside_ must be made of something _denser_ than rock.
2) _Meteorites_ which crash to Earth are often made of _iron and nickel_.
3) Iron and nickel are both _magnetic_ and very _dense_.
4) So if the _CORE_ of the Earth were made of _iron and nickel_ it would explain a lot, i.e. the _high density_ of the Earth and the fact that it has a _magnetic field_ round it (see the Physics Book).
5) Also, by following the paths of _seismic waves_ from earthquakes as they travel through the Earth, we can tell that there is a _change_ to _liquid_ about _halfway_ through the Earth.
6) Hence we deduce a _liquid outer core of iron and nickel_. The seismic waves also indicate a solid inner core (see Physics Book). See how very easy it all is when you know.

The Earth's Surface is made up of Large Plates of Rock

1) These _plates_ are like _big rafts_ that float across the liquid mantle.

2) The map shows the _edges_ of these plates. As they _move_, the _continents_ move too.

3) The plates are moving at a speed of about _1cm or 2cm per year_.

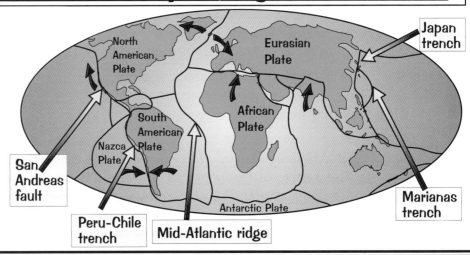

North American Plate

Eurasian Plate

Japan trench

African Plate

South American Plate

Nazca Plate

San Andreas fault

Peru-Chile trench

Mid-Atlantic ridge

Antarctic Plate

Marianas trench

Try Telling that lot to the Spanish Inquisition...

More _nice easy stuff_. That means it's nice easy marks in the Exam too. They do put easy stuff in, just so that everyone gets at least some marks. Just make sure you learn _ALL_ the details. There's _nothing dafter_ than missing easy marks. _Cover the page and check you know it ALL_.

Evidence for Plate Tectonics

Crinkly bits from Cooling? — I don't think so, matey

The _old theory_ was that all the _features_ of the Earth's surface, e.g. mountains, were due to _shrinkage_ of the crust as it _cooled_. In the Exam they may well ask you about that, and then they'll ask you for _evidence_ in favour of _plate tectonics_ as a _better theory_. Learn and prosper:

1) Jigsaw Fit — the supercontinent "Pangaea"

a) There's a very obvious _jigsaw fit_ between _Africa_ and _South America_.

b) The _other continents_ can _also_ be fitted in without too much trouble.

c) It's widely believed that they once all formed _a single land mass_, now called _Pangea_.

2) Matching Fossils in Africa and South America

a) Identical _plant fossils_ of the _same age_ have been found in rocks in _South Africa_, _Australia_, _Antarctica_, _India_ and _South America_, which strongly suggests they were all _joined_ once upon a time.

b) _Animal fossils_ support the theory too. There are identical fossils of a _freshwater crocodile_ found in both _Brazil_ and _South Africa_. It certainly didn't swim across.

Identical fossils of the same freshwater crocodile found in both <u>South America</u> and <u>South Africa</u>

3) Living Creatures: The Earthworm

a) There are various _living creatures_ found in _both_ America and Africa.

b) One such beasty is a particular _earthworm_ which is found living at the _tip of South America_ and the _tip of South Africa_.

c) How come? Well most likely it travelled across _ever so slowly_ on the big raft we now call America.

Well! I warned you...

America   Africa

4) Identical Rock Sequences

a) When _rock strata_ of similar _ages_ are studied in various countries they show remarkable _similarity_.

b) This is strong evidence that these countries were _joined together_ when the rocks _formed_.

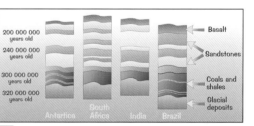

200 000 000 years old
240 000 000 years old
300 000 000 years old
320 000 000 years old

Basalt
Sandstones
Coals and shales
Glacial deposits

Antartica   South Africa   India   Brazil

5) Magnetic Stripes in the Ocean Floor (See P. 53 for fuller details on this.)

a) The _symmetrical pattern_ of _magnetic "stripes"_ in the rocks on either side of the _mid-Atlantic ridge_ is the clearest evidence of all that the two sides are _spreading_ away from each other.

b) These magnetic stripes were only discovered in the 1960s.

N S N S N S

Magma

Learn about Plate Tectonics — but don't get carried away...

Five bits of evidence which support the theory that there are big plates of rock moving about. Learn all five well enough to be able to answer a question like this: "Describe evidence which supports the theory of Plate Tectonics" (5 marks). _Learn, cover, scribble, etc..._

Plate Boundaries

At the _boundaries_ between tectonic plates there's usually _trouble_ like _volcanoes_ or _earthquakes_.
There are _three_ different ways that plates interact: _Colliding_, _separating_ or _sliding_ past each other.

Oceanic and Continental Plates Colliding: The Andes

1) The _oceanic plate_ is always _forced underneath_ the continental plate.
2) This is called a _subduction zone_.
3) As the oceanic crust is pushed down it _melts_ and _pressure builds up_ due to all the melting rock.
4) This _molten rock_ finds its way to the _surface_ and _volcanoes_ form.
5) There are also _earthquakes_ as the two plates slowly _grind_ past each other.
6) A _deep trench_ forms on the ocean floor where the _oceanic plate_ is being _forced down_.
7) The _continental_ crust _crumples_ and _folds_ forming _mountains_ at the coast.
8) The classic example of all this is the _west coast of South America_ where the _Andes mountains_ are. That region has _all the features_:

Volcanoes, _earthquakes_, an _oceanic trench_ and _mountains_.

Two Continental Plates Collide: The Himalayas

1) The _two continental plates_ meet _head on_, neither one being subducted.
2) Any _sediment layers_ lying between the two continent masses get _squeezed_ between them.
3) These sediment layers inevitably start _crumpling and folding_ and soon form into _big mountains_.
4) The _Himalayan mountains_ are the classic case of this.

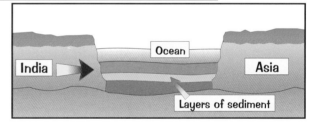

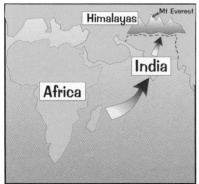

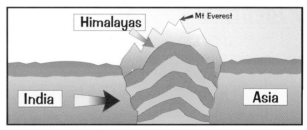

5) _India_ actually _broke away_ from the side of Africa and _piled_ into the bottom of _Asia_, and is _still_ doing so, _pushing the Himalayas up_ as it goes.
6) _Mount Everest_ is there and is _getting higher_ by a few cm every year as India continues to push up into the continent of Asia.

Another page to learn — don't make a mountain out of it...

Make sure you learn all these diagrams — they summarise all the information in the text.
They may well ask you for examples in the Exam, so make sure you know the two different kinds of situation that the Andes and the Himalayas actually represent. _Cover and scribble..._

Plate Boundaries

Sea Floor Spreading: The Mid-Atlantic Ridge

1) When tectonic plates move *apart*, *magma rises up* to fill the gap and produces *new crust* made of *basalt* (of course). Sometimes it comes out with *great force* producing *undersea volcanoes*.
2) The *Mid-Atlantic ridge* runs the *whole length* of the Atlantic and actually cuts through the middle of *Iceland*, which is why they have *hot underground water*.
3) As the magma rises up through the gap it forms *ridges* and *underwater mountains*.
4) These form a *symmetrical pattern* either side of the ridge, providing strong *evidence* for the theory of *continental drift*.
5) However the most *compelling* evidence comes from the *magnetic orientation* of the rocks.
6) As the *liquid magma* erupts out of the gap, the *iron particles* in the rocks tend to *align themselves* with the *Earth's magnetic field* and as it cools they *set* in position.
7) Every half million years or so the Earth's magnetic field tends to *swap direction*.
8) This means the rock on *either side of the ridge* has bands of *alternate magnetic polarity*.
9) This pattern is found to be *symmetrical* either side of the ridge.

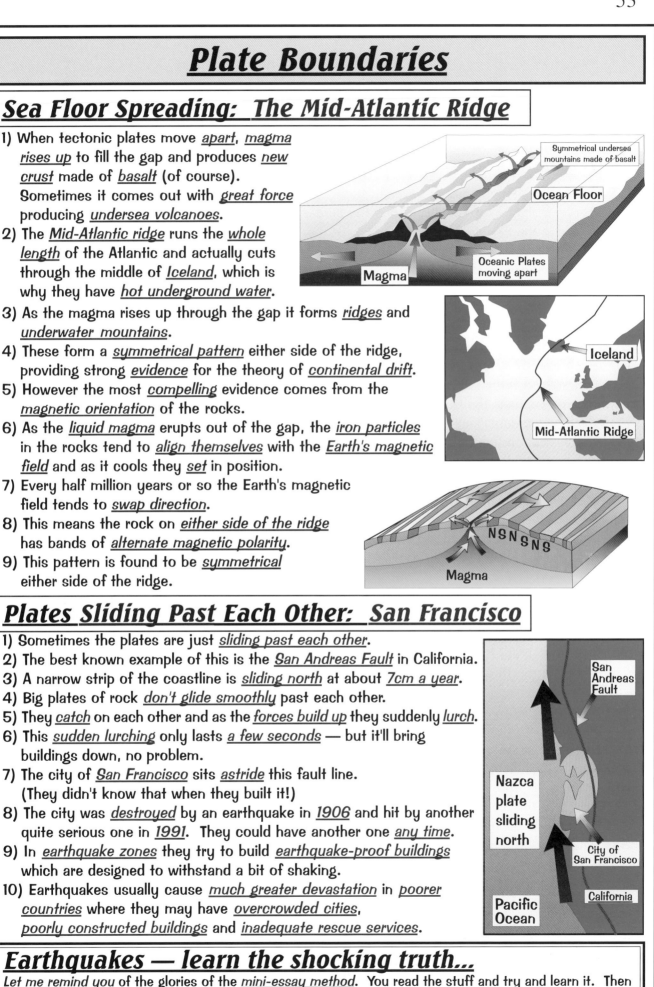

Plates Sliding Past Each Other: San Francisco

1) Sometimes the plates are just *sliding past each other*.
2) The best known example of this is the *San Andreas Fault* in California.
3) A narrow strip of the coastline is *sliding north* at about *7cm a year*.
4) Big plates of rock *don't glide smoothly* past each other.
5) They *catch* on each other and as the *forces build up* they suddenly *lurch*.
6) This *sudden lurching* only lasts *a few seconds* — but it'll bring buildings down, no problem.
7) The city of *San Francisco* sits *astride* this fault line. (They didn't know that when they built it!)
8) The city was *destroyed* by an earthquake in *1906* and hit by another quite serious one in *1991*. They could have another one *any time*.
9) In *earthquake zones* they try to build *earthquake-proof buildings* which are designed to withstand a bit of shaking.
10) Earthquakes usually cause *much greater devastation* in *poorer countries* where they may have *overcrowded cities*, *poorly constructed buildings* and *inadequate rescue services*.

Earthquakes — learn the shocking truth...

Let me remind you of the glories of the *mini-essay method*. You read the stuff and try and learn it. Then you cover the page and scribble yourself a mini-essay on each topic. Then you look back and see what stuff you missed. *Then you try again, and again — until you get it ALL.* Glorious. Isn't it...

Revision Summary For Section Four

Well let's face it, this section on Air and Rock is definitely the easy interlude in the Chemistry syllabus. In the Olden Days (the 1970s) this stuff all used to be called Geography, which as you know, is a much easier subject than Chemistry. However, easy or not, there's still quite a lot of stuff to learn. Try these little jokers and see how much you know:

1) What are the percentages of gases in today's atmosphere?
2) Describe a simple experiment to find the percentage of oxygen in air.
3) How old is the Earth? What was it like for the first billion years or so?
4) What gases did the early atmosphere consist of? Where did these gases come from?
5) What was the main thing which caused phase two of the atmosphere's evolution?
6) Which gases became much less common and which one increased?
7) Which gas allowed phase three to take place? Which gas is almost completely gone?
8) Explain how the oceans contain carbon.
9) What are the three man-made atmospheric problems?
10) Which gases cause acid rain? Where do they come from?
    What are the three adverse effects of acid rain?
11) Which gas causes the Greenhouse effect? Explain how the Greenhouse effect works.
12) Which gas is damaging the ozone layer? What are the harmful effects of this?
13) What is the "carbon cycle" concerned with?
14) Draw out the diagram of the Carbon Cycle from memory.
15) What are the three types of weathering? Explain the details for each type, with diagrams.
16) What exactly is "erosion"? What process is "transport"?
17) Which of these processes created the Grand Canyon or any other river valley?
18) Draw a pretty diagram of the water cycle. Explain how the whole process works.
19) What are the three types of rock? Draw a full diagram of the rock cycle.
20) Explain how the three types of rock change from one to another. How long does this take?
21) Draw diagrams to show how sedimentary rocks form.
22) What are found in sedimentary rocks but are not found in any other type of rock?
23) List the four main sedimentary rocks, give a description of each, and a use for two of them.
24) Draw a diagram to show how metamorphic rocks are formed. What does the name mean?
25) What are the three main metamorphic rocks?
    Describe their appearance and give a use for two of them.
26) How are igneous rocks formed? What are the two types? Give an example of each.
27) What is the difference in the way that they formed and in their structure and appearance?
28) Draw a diagram of the internal structure of the Earth, with labels.
29) How big are the various parts in relation to each other? What is the mantle made of?
30) What is the core made of? What are the three big clues that tell us about the Earth?
31) What was the old theory about the Earth's surface? What is the theory of Plate Tectonics?
32) Give details of the five bits of evidence which support the theory of Plate Tectonics.
33) What are the three different ways that tectonic plates interact at boundaries?
34) What happens when an oceanic plate collides with a continental plate? Draw a diagram.
35) What four features does this produce? Which part of the world is the classic case of this?
36) What happens when two continental plates collide? Draw diagrams.
37) What features does this produce? Which part of the world is the classic case of this?
38) What is the Mid-Atlantic ridge? What happens there?
39) Which country lies on top of it? Do they suffer earthquakes? What *do* they get?
40) Where is the San Andreas fault? What are the tectonic plates doing along this fault line?
41) Why does it cause Earthquakes — and why did they build San Francisco right on top of it?

A Brief History of The Periodic Table

The early Chemists were keen to try and find _patterns_ in the elements.
The _more_ elements that were identified, the _easier_ it became to find patterns of course.

In the Early 1800s They Could Only go on Atomic Mass

They had _two_ obvious ways to categorise elements:

1) Their _physical_ and _chemical properties_	2) Their _Relative Atomic Mass_

1) Remember, they had _no idea_ of _atomic structure_ or of protons or electrons, so there was _no such thing_ as _atomic number_ to them. (It was only in the 20th century after protons and electrons were discovered, that it was realised the elements should be arranged in order of _atomic number_.)
2) But _back then_, the only thing they could measure was _Relative Atomic Mass_ and the only obvious way to arrange the known elements was _in order of atomic mass_.
3) When this was done a _periodic pattern_ was noticed in the _properties_ of the elements.

Newlands' Octaves Were The First Good Effort

A chap called _Newlands_ had the first good stab at it in _1863_. He noticed that every _eighth_ element had similar properties and so he listed some of the known elements in rows of seven:

Li	Be	B	C	N	O	F
Na	Mg	Al	Si	P	S	Cl

These sets of eight were called _Newlands' Octaves_ but unfortunately the pattern _broke down_ on the _third row_ with many _transition metals_ like Fe and Cu and Zn messing it up completely.
It was because _he left no gaps_ that his work was _ignored_.
But he was getting _pretty close_ as you can see.

Dmitri Mendeleev Left Gaps and Predicted New Elements

1) In _1869_, _Dmitri Mendeleev_ in Russia, armed with about 50 known elements, arranged them into his Table of Elements with various _gaps_, as shown.
2) Mendeleev ordered the elements in order of _atomic mass_ (like Newlands did).
3) But Mendeleev found he had to leave _gaps_ in order to keep elements with _similar properties_ in the same _vertical groups_ — and he was prepared to leave some _very big gaps_ in the first two rows before the transition metals come in on the _third_ row.

The _gaps_ were the really clever bit because they _predicted_ the properties of so far _undiscovered elements_.

When they were found and they _fitted the pattern_ it was pretty smashing news for old Dmitri. The old rogue.

Mendeleev's Table of the Elements

```
H
Li  Be                                              B   C   N   O   F
Na  Mg                                              Al  Si  P   S   Cl
K   Ca  *     Ti  V   Cr  Mn  Fe  Co  Ni  Cu  Zn  *   *   As  Se  Br
Rb  Sr  Y     Zr  Nb  Mo  *   Ru  Rh  Pd  Ag  Cd  In  Sn  Sb  Te  I
Cs  Ba  *   *  Ta  W   *   Os  Ir  Pt  Au  Hg  Tl  Pb  Bi
```

I Can't see what all the fuss is — it all seems quite elementary...

They're quite into having bits of History in Science now. They like to think you'll gain an appreciation of the role of science in the overall progress of human society. Personally, I'm not that bothered whether you do or not. All I wanna know is: _Have you learnt all the facts yet?_ And if not — _WHY NOT? HUH?_

The Periodic Table

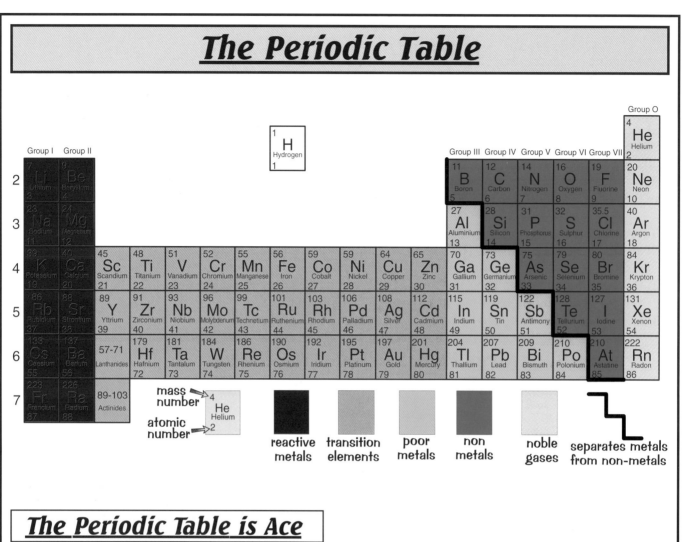

The Periodic Table is Ace

1) The _modern_ Periodic Table shows the elements in order of _atomic number_.
2) The Periodic Table is laid out so that elements with _similar properties_ form in _columns_.
3) These _vertical columns_ are called _Groups_ and Roman Numerals are often used for them.
4) For example the _Group II_ elements are Be, Mg, Ca, Sr, Ba and Ra.
   They're all _metals_ which form 2+ ions and they have many other _similar properties_.
5) The _rows_ are called _periods_.
6) Each _new period_ represents _another full shell_ of electrons.

The Elements of a Group Have the Same Outer Electrons

1) The elements in each _Group_ all have the same number of _electrons_ in their _outer shell_.
2) That's why they have _similar properties_. And that's why we arrange them in this way.
3) You absolutely must get that into your head if you want to _understand_ any Chemistry.
4) The properties of the elements are decided _entirely_ by how many electrons they have.
5) So the _atomic number_ of an atom is really significant because it's equal to how many electrons the atom has.
6) But don't forget, it's the number of electrons in the _outer shell_ which is the really important thing.

Electron Shells — where would we be without them...

Make sure you learn the whole periodic table including every name, symbol and number.
No, only kidding! Just _learn_ the numbered points and _scribble_ them down, _mini-essay style_.

Electron Arrangements

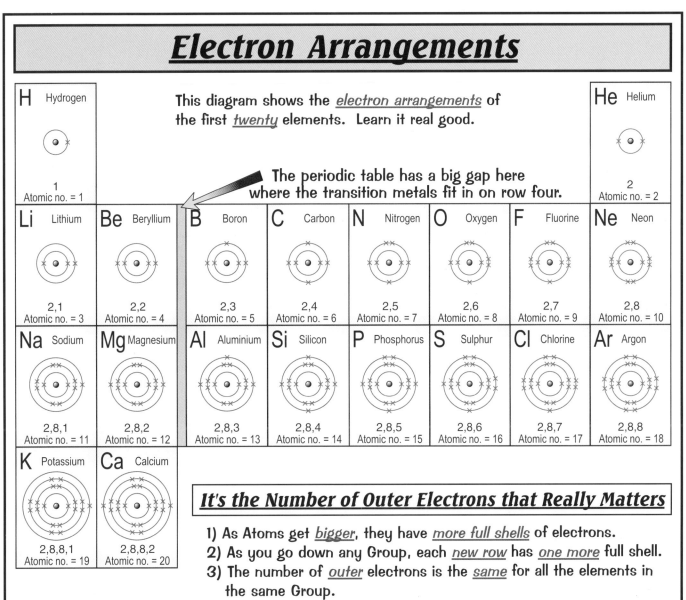

This diagram shows the *electron arrangements* of the first *twenty* elements. Learn it real good.

The periodic table has a big gap here where the transition metals fit in on row four.

It's the Number of Outer Electrons that Really Matters

1) As Atoms get *bigger*, they have *more full shells* of electrons.
2) As you go down any Group, each *new row* has *one more* full shell.
3) The number of *outer* electrons is the *same* for all the elements in the same Group.

Electron Shells are just Totally Brill

1) The fact that electrons form shells around atoms is the reason for the whole of chemistry.
2) If they just whizzed around the nucleus any old how and didn't care about shells or any of that stuff there'd be no chemical reactions.
3) No nothing in fact — because nothing would happen.
4) Without shells there'd be no atoms wanting to gain, lose or share electrons to form full shell arrangements.
5) So they wouldn't be interested in forming ions or covalent bonds. Nothing would bother and nothing would happen. The atoms would just slob about, all day long. Just like teenagers.
6) But amazingly, they *do* form shells (if they didn't, we wouldn't even be here to wonder about it), and the electron arrangement of each atom determines the whole of its chemical behaviour.
7) Phew. I mean electron arrangements explain practically the whole Universe.
They're just totally brill.

Electron Shells — aren't they just brill...

Really, you should know enough about electron shells to do that whole diagram at the top of the page without looking at it. Obviously you don't learn every atom separately — you learn the pattern. *Then cover the page and see what you know — by scribbling.*

Group O — The Noble Gases

	Group VI	Group VII	Group O
			4 **He** Helium 2
	O	F	20 **Ne** Neon 10
	S	Cl	40 **Ar** Argon 18
	Se	Br	84 **Kr** Krypton 36
	Te	I	131 **Xe** Xenon 54
	Po	At	222 **Rn** Radon 86

As you go down the Group:

1) The density increases
because the atomic mass increases.

2) The boiling point increases
Helium boils at –269°C (that's cold!)
Xenon boils at –108°C (that's still cold).

They all have full outer shells — That's why they're so inert

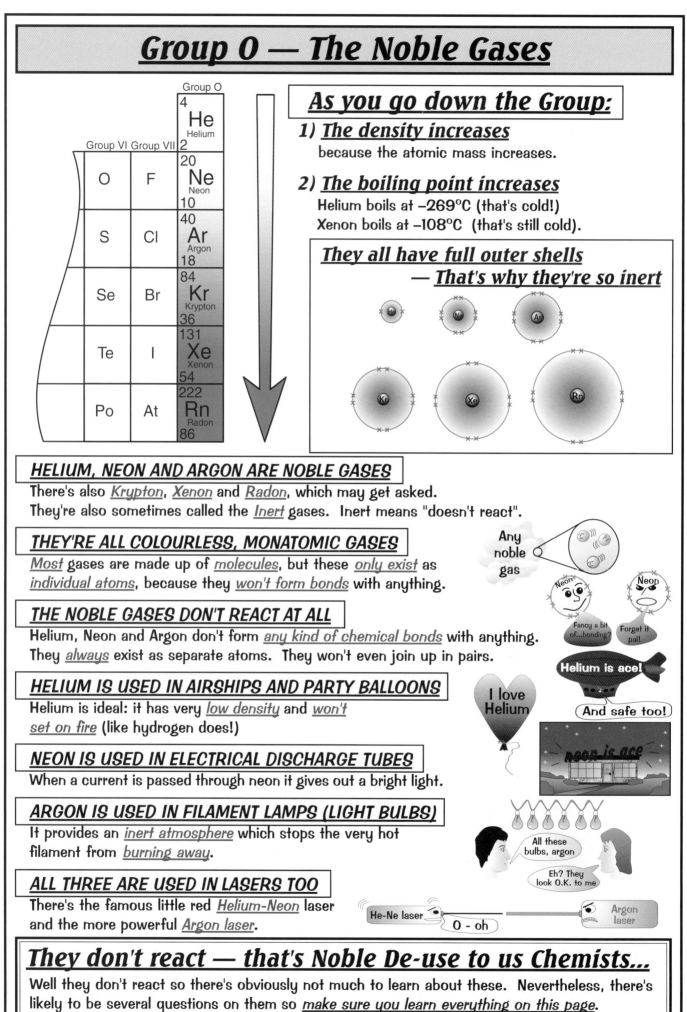

HELIUM, NEON AND ARGON ARE NOBLE GASES
There's also _Krypton_, _Xenon_ and _Radon_, which may get asked.
They're also sometimes called the _Inert_ gases. Inert means "doesn't react".

THEY'RE ALL COLOURLESS, MONATOMIC GASES
Most gases are made up of _molecules_, but these _only exist_ as
individual atoms, because they _won't form bonds_ with anything.

THE NOBLE GASES DON'T REACT AT ALL
Helium, Neon and Argon don't form _any kind of chemical bonds_ with anything.
They _always_ exist as separate atoms. They won't even join up in pairs.

Any noble gas

Neon — Fancy a bit of...bonding?
Neon — Forget it pal!

HELIUM IS USED IN AIRSHIPS AND PARTY BALLOONS
Helium is ideal: it has very _low density_ and _won't
set on fire_ (like hydrogen does!)

I love Helium

Helium is ace!
And safe too!

NEON IS USED IN ELECTRICAL DISCHARGE TUBES
When a current is passed through neon it gives out a bright light.

neon is ace

ARGON IS USED IN FILAMENT LAMPS (LIGHT BULBS)
It provides an _inert atmosphere_ which stops the very hot
filament from _burning away_.

All these bulbs, argon
Eh? They look O.K. to me

ALL THREE ARE USED IN LASERS TOO
There's the famous little red _Helium-Neon_ laser
and the more powerful _Argon laser_.

He-Ne laser   O - oh   Argon laser

They don't react — that's Noble De-use to us Chemists...
Well they don't react so there's obviously not much to learn about these. Nevertheless, there's
likely to be several questions on them so _make sure you learn everything on this page_.

Group I — The Alkali Metals

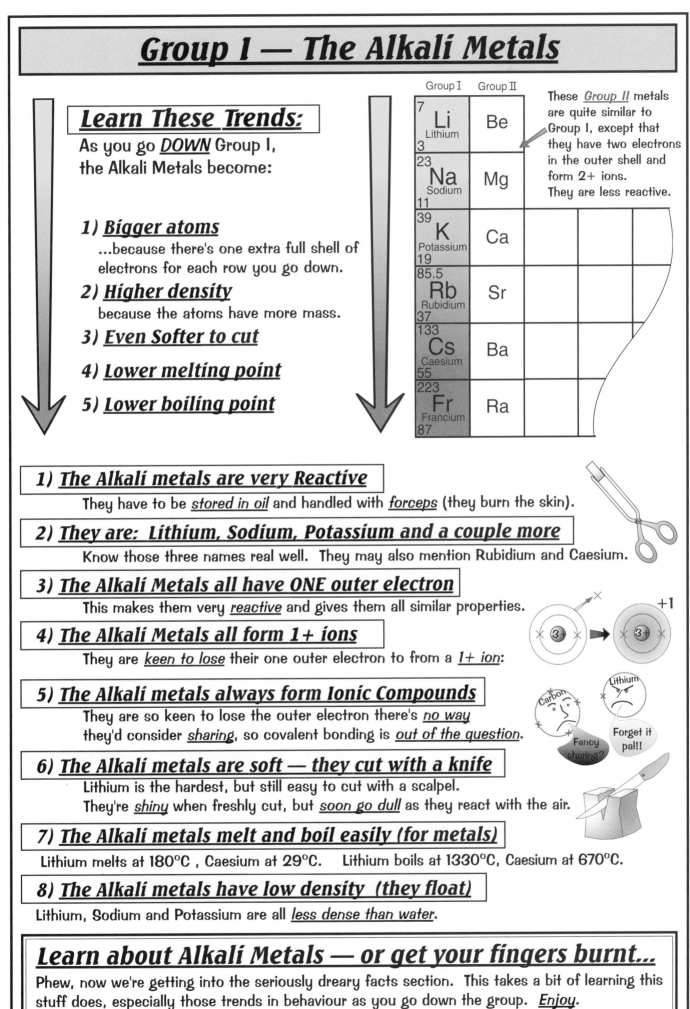

Learn These Trends:

As you go *DOWN* Group I,
the Alkali Metals become:

1) Bigger atoms
...because there's one extra full shell of electrons for each row you go down.

2) Higher density
because the atoms have more mass.

3) Even Softer to cut

4) Lower melting point

5) Lower boiling point

Group I	Group II
7 Li Lithium 3	Be
23 Na Sodium 11	Mg
39 K Potassium 19	Ca
85.5 Rb Rubidium 37	Sr
133 Cs Caesium 55	Ba
223 Fr Francium 87	Ra

These *Group II* metals are quite similar to Group I, except that they have two electrons in the outer shell and form 2+ ions.
They are less reactive.

1) The Alkali metals are very Reactive
They have to be *stored in oil* and handled with *forceps* (they burn the skin).

2) They are: Lithium, Sodium, Potassium and a couple more
Know those three names real well. They may also mention Rubidium and Caesium.

3) The Alkali Metals all have ONE outer electron
This makes them very *reactive* and gives them all similar properties.

4) The Alkali Metals all form 1+ ions
They are *keen to lose* their one outer electron to from a *1+ ion*:

5) The Alkali metals always form Ionic Compounds
They are so keen to lose the outer electron there's *no way* they'd consider *sharing*, so covalent bonding is *out of the question*.

6) The Alkali metals are soft — they cut with a knife
Lithium is the hardest, but still easy to cut with a scalpel.
They're *shiny* when freshly cut, but *soon go dull* as they react with the air.

7) The Alkali metals melt and boil easily (for metals)
Lithium melts at 180°C , Caesium at 29°C.   Lithium boils at 1330°C, Caesium at 670°C.

8) The Alkali metals have low density (they float)
Lithium, Sodium and Potassium are all *less dense than water*.

Learn about Alkali Metals — or get your fingers burnt...
Phew, now we're getting into the seriously dreary facts section. This takes a bit of learning this stuff does, especially those trends in behaviour as you go down the group. *Enjoy.*

Reactions of the Alkali Metals

Reaction with Cold Water produces Hydrogen Gas

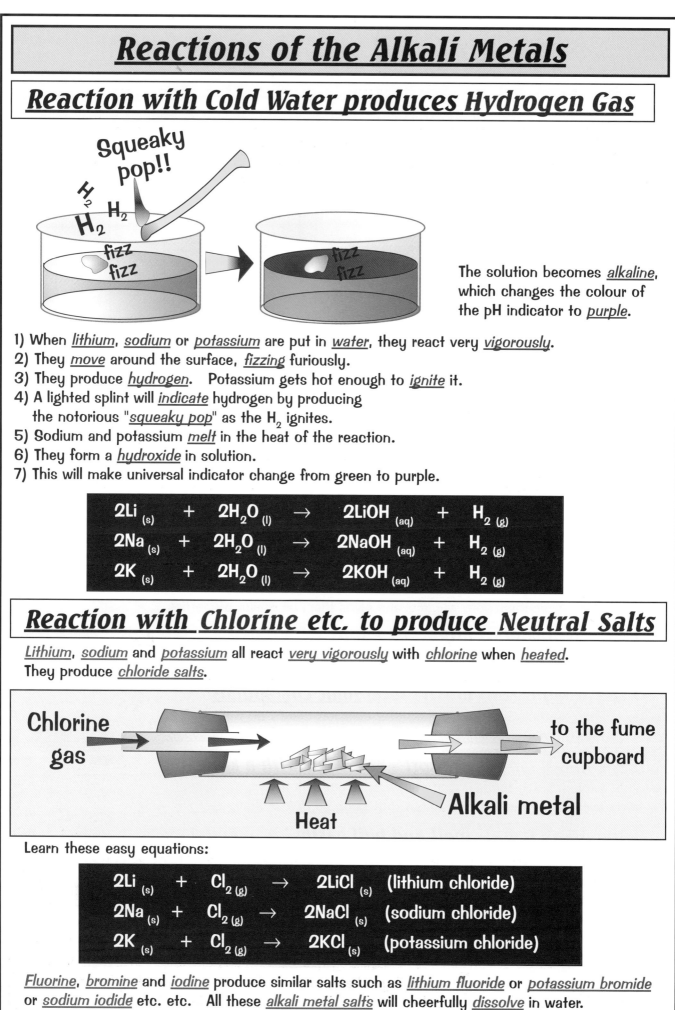

The solution becomes _alkaline_, which changes the colour of the pH indicator to _purple_.

1) When _lithium_, _sodium_ or _potassium_ are put in _water_, they react very _vigorously_.
2) They _move_ around the surface, _fizzing_ furiously.
3) They produce _hydrogen_. Potassium gets hot enough to _ignite_ it.
4) A lighted splint will _indicate_ hydrogen by producing the notorious "_squeaky pop_" as the H_2 ignites.
5) Sodium and potassium _melt_ in the heat of the reaction.
6) They form a _hydroxide_ in solution.
7) This will make universal indicator change from green to purple.

$$2Li_{(s)} + 2H_2O_{(l)} \rightarrow 2LiOH_{(aq)} + H_{2(g)}$$
$$2Na_{(s)} + 2H_2O_{(l)} \rightarrow 2NaOH_{(aq)} + H_{2(g)}$$
$$2K_{(s)} + 2H_2O_{(l)} \rightarrow 2KOH_{(aq)} + H_{2(g)}$$

Reaction with Chlorine etc. to produce Neutral Salts

Lithium, _sodium_ and _potassium_ all react _very vigorously_ with _chlorine_ when _heated_. They produce _chloride salts_.

Chlorine gas

to the fume cupboard

Alkali metal

Heat

Learn these easy equations:

$$2Li_{(s)} + Cl_{2(g)} \rightarrow 2LiCl_{(s)} \text{ (lithium chloride)}$$
$$2Na_{(s)} + Cl_{2(g)} \rightarrow 2NaCl_{(s)} \text{ (sodium chloride)}$$
$$2K_{(s)} + Cl_{2(g)} \rightarrow 2KCl_{(s)} \text{ (potassium chloride)}$$

Fluorine, _bromine_ and _iodine_ produce similar salts such as _lithium fluoride_ or _potassium bromide_ or _sodium iodide_ etc. etc. All these _alkali metal salts_ will cheerfully _dissolve_ in water.

Reactions of the Alkali Metals

Alkali Metals burn in Air to produce Oxides

All the alkali metals *burn in air* and in the process turn into oxides.
You ought to be able to repeat these easy equations with no more effort than a mere flick of the pencil:

$$4Li_{(s)} + O_{2(g)} \rightarrow 2Li_2O_{(s)} \text{ (lithium oxide)}$$

$$4Na_{(s)} + O_{2(g)} \rightarrow 2Na_2O_{(s)} \text{ (sodium oxide)}$$

$$4K_{(s)} + O_{2(g)} \rightarrow 2K_2O_{(s)} \text{ (potassium oxide)}$$

They all *burn in air* with *pretty coloured flames*:

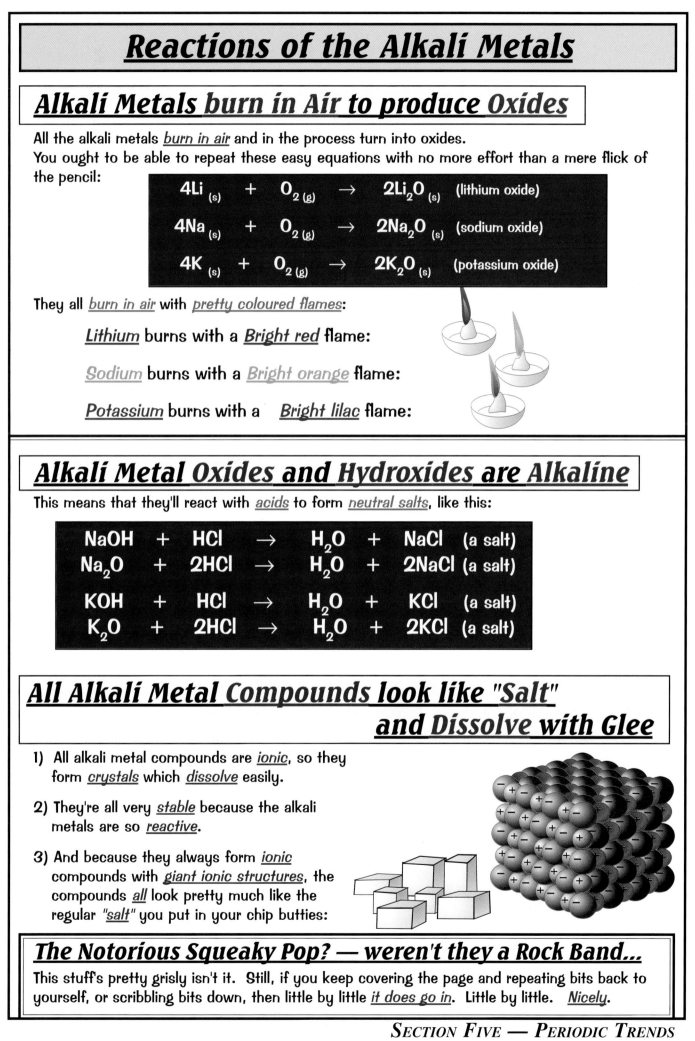

    Lithium burns with a *Bright red* flame:

    Sodium burns with a *Bright orange* flame:

    Potassium burns with a   *Bright lilac* flame:

Alkali Metal Oxides and Hydroxides are Alkaline

This means that they'll react with *acids* to form *neutral salts*, like this:

$$NaOH + HCl \rightarrow H_2O + NaCl \text{ (a salt)}$$
$$Na_2O + 2HCl \rightarrow H_2O + 2NaCl \text{ (a salt)}$$

$$KOH + HCl \rightarrow H_2O + KCl \text{ (a salt)}$$
$$K_2O + 2HCl \rightarrow H_2O + 2KCl \text{ (a salt)}$$

All Alkali Metal Compounds look like "Salt" and Dissolve with Glee

1) All alkali metal compounds are *ionic*, so they form *crystals* which *dissolve* easily.

2) They're all very *stable* because the alkali metals are so *reactive*.

3) And because they always form *ionic* compounds with *giant ionic structures*, the compounds *all* look pretty much like the regular *"salt"* you put in your chip butties:

The Notorious Squeaky Pop? — weren't they a Rock Band...

This stuff's pretty grisly isn't it. Still, if you keep covering the page and repeating bits back to yourself, or scribbling bits down, then little by little *it does go in*. Little by little. *Nicely.*

Group VII — The Halogens

Learn These Trends:

As you go _DOWN_ Group VII, the _HALOGENS_ become:

1) Bigger atoms
...because there's one extra full shell of electrons for each row you go down.

2) Less Reactive
...because there's less inclination to gain the extra electron to fill the outer shell when it's further out from the nucleus.

3) Darker in colour

4) They go from gas to solid
Fluorine and _chlorine_ are _gases_, _bromine_ is a _liquid_, and _iodine_ is a _solid_.

5) Higher melting point

6) Higher boiling point

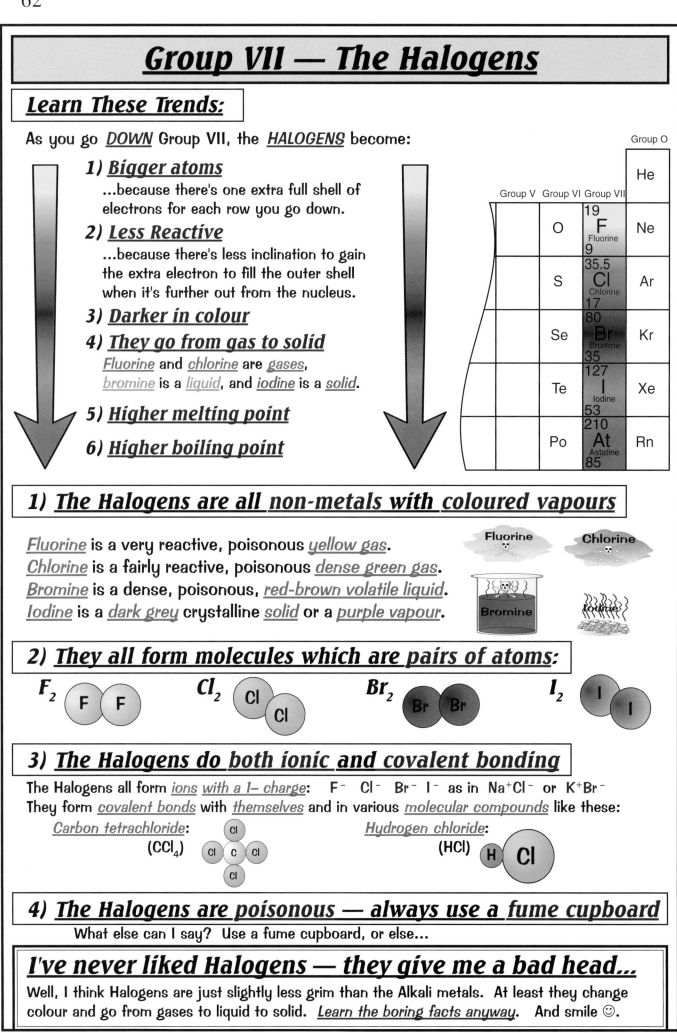

Group V	Group VI	Group VII	Group O
			He
O	$\begin{array}{c}19\\ F\\ \text{Fluorine}\\ 9\end{array}$		Ne
S	$\begin{array}{c}35.5\\ Cl\\ \text{Chlorine}\\ 17\end{array}$		Ar
Se	$\begin{array}{c}80\\ Br\\ \text{Bromine}\\ 35\end{array}$		Kr
Te	$\begin{array}{c}127\\ I\\ \text{Iodine}\\ 53\end{array}$		Xe
Po	$\begin{array}{c}210\\ At\\ \text{Astatine}\\ 85\end{array}$		Rn

1) The Halogens are all non-metals with coloured vapours

Fluorine is a very reactive, poisonous _yellow gas_.
Chlorine is a fairly reactive, poisonous _dense green gas_.
Bromine is a dense, poisonous, _red-brown volatile liquid_.
Iodine is a _dark grey_ crystalline _solid_ or a _purple vapour_.

2) They all form molecules which are pairs of atoms:

F_2 F F Cl_2 Cl Cl Br_2 Br Br I_2 I I

3) The Halogens do both ionic and covalent bonding

The Halogens all form _ions with a 1− charge_: F^- Cl^- Br^- I^- as in Na^+Cl^- or K^+Br^-
They form _covalent bonds_ with _themselves_ and in various _molecular compounds_ like these:

Carbon tetrachloride: _Hydrogen chloride:_
(CCl_4) Cl Cl C Cl Cl   (HCl)   H Cl

4) The Halogens are poisonous — always use a fume cupboard

What else can I say? Use a fume cupboard, or else...

I've never liked Halogens — they give me a bad head...

Well, I think Halogens are just slightly less grim than the Alkali metals. At least they change colour and go from gases to liquid to solid. _Learn the boring facts anyway._ And smile ☺.

Reactions of The Halogens

1) The Halogens react with metals to form salts

They _react_ with most _metals_ including _iron_ and _aluminium_, to form _salts_ (or "_metal halides_").

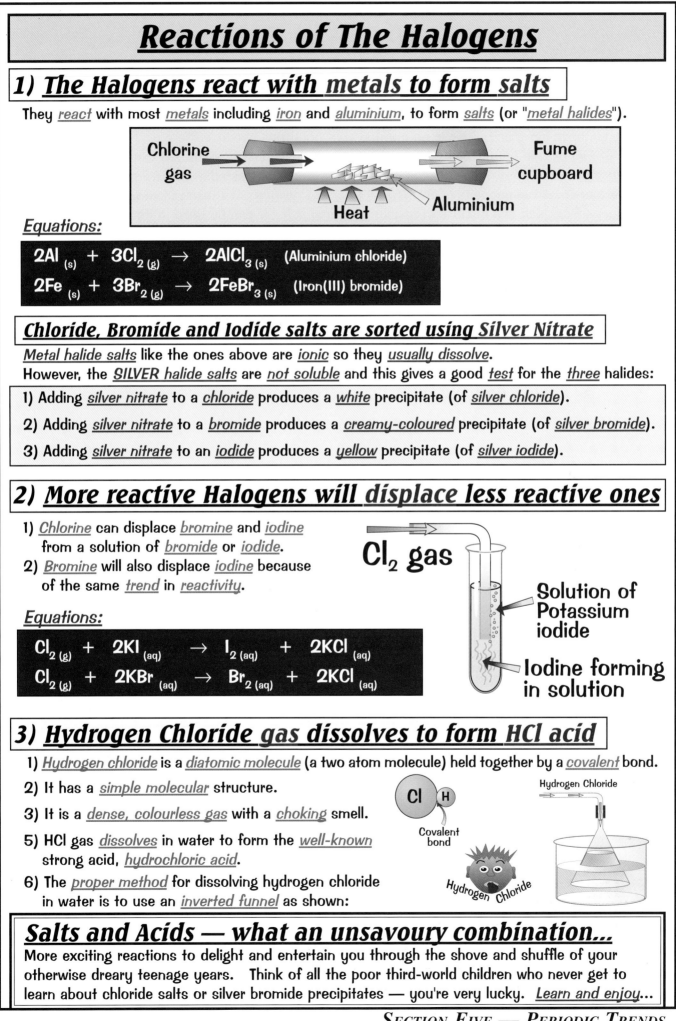

Equations:

$$2Al_{(s)} + 3Cl_{2(g)} \rightarrow 2AlCl_{3(s)} \quad \text{(Aluminium chloride)}$$
$$2Fe_{(s)} + 3Br_{2(g)} \rightarrow 2FeBr_{3(s)} \quad \text{(Iron(III) bromide)}$$

Chloride, Bromide and Iodide salts are sorted using Silver Nitrate

Metal halide salts like the ones above are _ionic_ so they _usually dissolve_.
However, the _SILVER halide salts_ are _not soluble_ and this gives a good _test_ for the _three_ halides:

1) Adding _silver nitrate_ to a _chloride_ produces a _white_ precipitate (of _silver chloride_).

2) Adding _silver nitrate_ to a _bromide_ produces a _creamy-coloured_ precipitate (of _silver bromide_).

3) Adding _silver nitrate_ to an _iodide_ produces a _yellow_ precipitate (of _silver iodide_).

2) More reactive Halogens will displace less reactive ones

1) _Chlorine_ can displace _bromine_ and _iodine_ from a solution of _bromide_ or _iodide_.

2) _Bromine_ will also displace _iodine_ because of the same _trend_ in _reactivity_.

Equations:

$$Cl_{2(g)} + 2KI_{(aq)} \rightarrow I_{2(aq)} + 2KCl_{(aq)}$$
$$Cl_{2(g)} + 2KBr_{(aq)} \rightarrow Br_{2(aq)} + 2KCl_{(aq)}$$

3) Hydrogen Chloride gas dissolves to form HCl acid

1) _Hydrogen chloride_ is a _diatomic molecule_ (a two atom molecule) held together by a _covalent_ bond.

2) It has a _simple molecular_ structure.

3) It is a _dense, colourless gas_ with a _choking_ smell.

5) HCl gas _dissolves_ in water to form the _well-known_ strong acid, _hydrochloric acid_.

6) The _proper method_ for dissolving hydrogen chloride in water is to use an _inverted funnel_ as shown:

Salts and Acids — what an unsavoury combination...

More exciting reactions to delight and entertain you through the shove and shuffle of your otherwise dreary teenage years.   Think of all the poor third-world children who never get to learn about chloride salts or silver bromide precipitates — you're very lucky. _Learn and enjoy..._

Industrial Salt

Salt is taken from the sea — and from underneath Cheshire

1) In *hot countries* they just pour *sea water* into *big flat open tanks* and let the *sun* evaporate the water to leave salt. This is no good in cold countries because there isn't enough sunshine.

2) In *Britain* (a cold country — as if you need reminding), salt is extracted from *underground deposits* left *millions of years* ago when *ancient seas* evaporated.
There are massive deposits of this *ROCK SALT* in *Cheshire*. It's taken from *underground mines*. Rock salt is a mixture of mainly *sand and salt*. It can be used in its *raw state* on roads, or the salt can be filtered out for more *refined uses*, as detailed below.

1) Rock salt is used for de-icing roads

1) The *salt* in the mixture *melts ice* by *lowering the freezing point* of water to around −5°C.
2) The *sand and grit* in it gives useful *grip* on ice which hasn't melted.

2) Salt (sodium chloride) is used in the food industry, somewhat

Salt is added to most *processed foods* to enhance the *flavour*.
It's now reckoned to be *unhealthy* to eat too much salt.

I'm just waiting for the great day of reckoning when finally every single food has been declared either generally unhealthy or else downright dangerous. Perhaps we should all lay bets on what'll be the last food still considered safe to eat. My money's on Dried Locusts.

3) Salt is used for making chemicals

Salt is important for the *chemicals industries*, which are mostly based around *Cheshire* and *Merseyside* because of all the *rock salt* there. The first thing they do is *electrolyse* it like this:

Electrolysis of Salt gives Hydrogen, Chlorine and NaOH

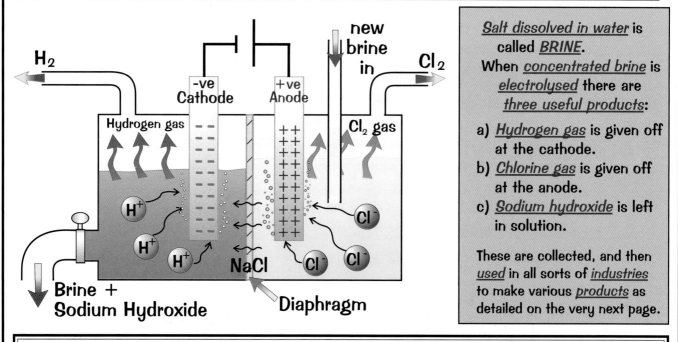

Salt dissolved in water is called *BRINE*.
When *concentrated brine* is *electrolysed* there are *three useful products*:

a) *Hydrogen gas* is given off at the cathode.
b) *Chlorine gas* is given off at the anode.
c) *Sodium hydroxide* is left in solution.

These are collected, and then *used* in all sorts of *industries* to make various *products* as detailed on the very next page.

Rock Salt — think of the pollution as it runs into the sea...

Look at this page. There's all that writing but only about *10 important facts to learn* in the whole lot. Hmm, I guess that's my fault — too much drivel. Still, if it makes you smile occasionally...

SECTION FIVE — PERIODIC TRENDS

Uses of Halogens and Salt Products

Some Uses of Halogens you Really Should Know

Fluorine, (or rather fluoride) reduces dental decay

Fluorides can be added to drinking water and toothpastes to help prevent tooth decay.

Chlorine is used in bleach and for sterilising water

1) Chlorine dissolved in sodium hydroxide solution is called bleach.
2) Chlorine compounds are also used to kill germs in swimming pools and drinking water.
3) It's also used to make insecticides and in the manufacture of HCl.

Iodine is used as an antiseptic...

...but it stings like nobody's business and stains the skin brown. Nice.

Silver halides are used on black and white photographic film

1) Silver is very unreactive. It does form halides but they're very easily split up.
2) In fact, ordinary visible light has enough energy to do so.
3) Photographic film is coated with colourless silver bromide.
4) When light hits parts of it, the silver bromide splits up into silver and bromine:

$$2AgBr \rightarrow Br_2 + 2Ag \text{ (silver metal)}$$

5) The silver metal appears black. The brighter the light, the darker it goes.
6) This produces a black and white negative, like an X-ray picture for example.

Useful Products from the Electrolysis of Brine

1) Chlorine

   1) Used in bleach, for sterilising water, for making HCl and insecticides.

2) Hydrogen

   1) Used in the Haber Process to make ammonia.
   2) Used to change oils into fats for making margarine. ("hydrogenated vegetable oil")

3) Sodium hydroxide

Sodium Hydroxide is a very strong alkali and is used widely in the chemical industry, e.g.
   1) soap   2) ceramics   3) organic chemicals   4) paper pulp   5) oven cleaner.

Sodium Carbonate from The Solvay Process

Salt is also used in the Solvay process for making sodium carbonate and sodium hydrogencarbonate which are two more useful chemicals you should maybe know about:

1) Sodium carbonate is used for:

   1) The manufacture of glass   2) Softening water.

2) Sodium hydrogencarbonate

This is also called sodium bicarbonate and it's used for baking cakes...(!)

Learn the many uses of salt — just use your brine...

Lots of seriously tedious facts to learn here. And virtually no nonsense. But think about it, the only bit you're gonna really remember forever is that bit about iodine. Am I right or am I right?

Acids and Alkalis

The pH Scale and Universal Indicator

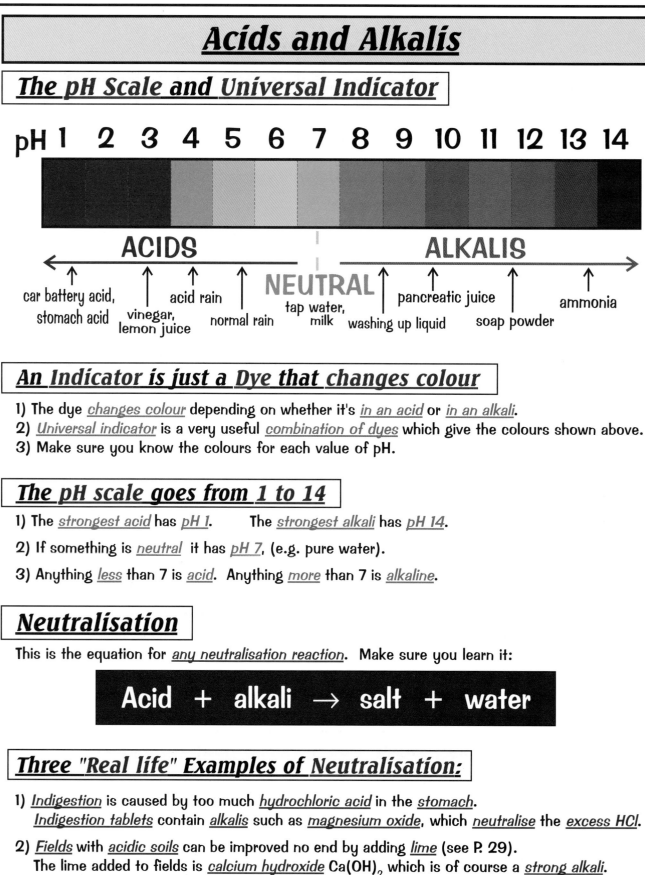

pH 1 2 3 4 5 6 7 8 9 10 11 12 13 14

← ACIDS   NEUTRAL   ALKALIS →

car battery acid, stomach acid | vinegar, lemon juice | acid rain | normal rain | tap water, milk | washing up liquid | pancreatic juice | soap powder | ammonia

An Indicator is just a Dye that changes colour

1) The dye *changes colour* depending on whether it's *in an acid* or *in an alkali*.
2) *Universal indicator* is a very useful *combination of dyes* which give the colours shown above.
3) Make sure you know the colours for each value of pH.

The pH scale goes from 1 to 14

1) The *strongest acid* has *pH 1*.   The *strongest alkali* has *pH 14*.

2) If something is *neutral* it has *pH 7*, (e.g. pure water).

3) Anything *less* than 7 is *acid*. Anything *more* than 7 is *alkaline*.

Neutralisation

This is the equation for *any neutralisation reaction*. Make sure you learn it:

$$\text{Acid} \ + \ \text{alkali} \ \rightarrow \ \text{salt} \ + \ \text{water}$$

Three "Real life" Examples of Neutralisation:

1) *Indigestion* is caused by too much *hydrochloric acid* in the *stomach*.
   Indigestion tablets contain *alkalis* such as *magnesium oxide*, which *neutralise* the *excess HCl*.

2) *Fields* with *acidic soils* can be improved no end by adding *lime* (see P. 29).
   The lime added to fields is *calcium hydroxide* $Ca(OH)_2$ which is of course a *strong alkali*.

3) *Lakes* affected by *acid rain* can also be *neutralised* by adding *lime*. This saves the fish.

Hey man, like "acid", yeah — eeuuucch...

Try and enjoy this page on acids and alkalis, because it gets *really* tedious from now on. These are very basic facts and possibly quite interesting. *Cover the page and scribble them down.*

SECTION FIVE — PERIODIC TRENDS

Acids Reacting With Metals

Acid + Metal → Salt + Hydrogen

That's written big 'cos it's kinda worth remembering.   Here's the _typical experiment_:

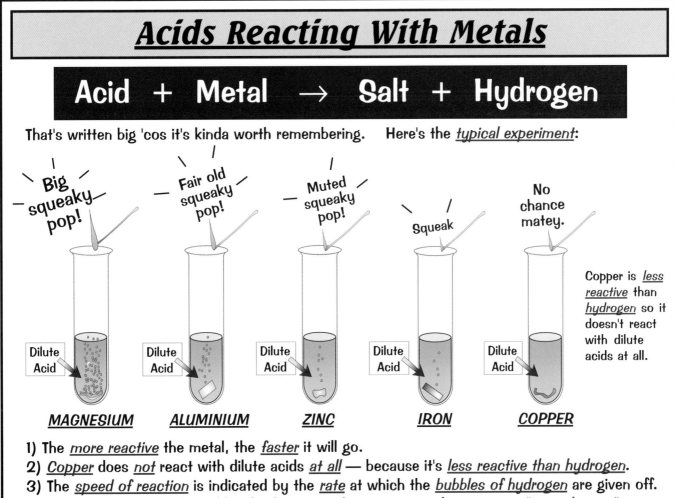

- \ Big squeaky pop! /
- \ Fair old squeaky pop! /
- \ Muted squeaky pop! /
- \ Squeak /
- No chance matey.

Copper is _less reactive_ than _hydrogen_ so it doesn't react with dilute acids at all.

Dilute Acid — **MAGNESIUM**   Dilute Acid — **ALUMINIUM**   Dilute Acid — **ZINC**   Dilute Acid — **IRON**   Dilute Acid — **COPPER**

1) The _more reactive_ the metal, the _faster_ it will go.
2) _Copper_ does _not_ react with dilute acids _at all_ — because it's _less reactive than hydrogen_.
3) The _speed of reaction_ is indicated by the _rate_ at which the _bubbles of hydrogen_ are given off.
4) The _hydrogen_ is confirmed by the _burning splint test_ giving the notorious "_squeaky pop_".
5) The _type of salt_ produced depends on which _metal_ is used, and which _acid_ is used:

Hydrochloric acid will always produce chloride salts:

$2HCl + Mg \rightarrow MgCl_2 + H_2$ (Magnesium chloride)

$6HCl + 2Al \rightarrow 2AlCl_3 + 3H_2$ (Aluminium chloride)

$2HCl + Zn \rightarrow ZnCl_2 + H_2$ (Zinc chloride)

Sulphuric acid will always produce sulphate salts:

$H_2SO_4 + Mg \rightarrow MgSO_4 + H_2$ (Magnesium sulphate)

$3H_2SO_4 + 2Al \rightarrow Al_2(SO_4)_3 + 3H_2$ (Aluminium sulphate)

$H_2SO_4 + Zn \rightarrow ZnSO_4 + H_2$ (Zinc sulphate)

Nitric acid produces nitrate salts when NEUTRALISED, but...

Nitric acid reacts fine with alkalis, to produce nitrates, but it can play silly devils with metals and produce nitrogen oxides instead, so we'll ignore it here. Chemistry's a real messy subject sometimes, innit.

Revision of Acids and Metals — easy as squeaky pop...

Actually, this stuff isn't too bad I don't think. I mean it's _fairly_ interesting. Not quite in the same league as The Spice Girls, I grant you, but for Chemistry it's not bad at all. At least there's bubbles and flames and noise and that kinda thing. Anyway, _learn it, scribble it down, etc..._

Acids with Oxides and Hydroxides

Metal Oxides and Metal Hydroxides are Alkalis

1) Some _metal oxides_ and _metal hydroxides_ dissolve in _water_ to produce _alkaline_ solutions.
2) In other words, metal oxides and metal hydroxides are generally _alkalis_.
3) This means they'll _react with acids_ to form _a salt_ and _water_.
4) Even those that won't dissolve in water will still react with acid.

Acid + Metal Oxide → Salt + Water

Acid + Metal Hydroxide → Salt + Water

(These are _neutralisation reactions_ of course)

The Combination of Metal and Acid decides the Salt

This isn't exactly exciting but it's pretty easy, so try and get the hang of it:

Hydrochloric acid + Copper oxide → Copper chloride + water
Hydrochloric acid + Sodium hydroxide → Sodium chloride + water

Sulphuric acid + Zinc oxide → Zinc sulphate + water
Sulphuric acid + Calcium hydroxide → Calcium sulphate + water

Nitric acid + Magnesium oxide → Magnesium nitrate + water
Nitric acid + Potassium hydroxide → Potassium nitrate + water

The symbol equations are all pretty much the same. Here's two of them:

$$H_2SO_4 + ZnO \rightarrow ZnSO_4 + H_2O$$
$$HNO_3 + KOH \rightarrow KNO_3 + H_2O$$

The Oxides of non-metals are usually Acidic, not alkaline

1) The _best_ examples are the _oxides_ of these three non-metals: _carbon_, _sulphur_ and _nitrogen_.
2) _Carbon dioxide_ dissolves in water to form _carbonic acid_ which is a _weak acid_.
3) _Sulphur dioxide_ combines with water and O_2 to form _sulphuric acid_ which is a _strong acid_.
4) _Nitrogen dioxide_ dissolves in water to form _nitric acid_ which is a _strong acid_.
5) These three are all present in _acid rain_ of course.
6) The _carbonic acid_ is present in rain _anyway_, so even _ordinary_ rain is slightly acidic.

Remember the three examples:

Non-metal oxides are ACIDIC:
CARBON DIOXIDE   SULPHUR DIOXIDE   NITROGEN DIOXIDE

Acids are really dull, aren't they — learn and snore...

You've gotta be a pretty serious career chemist to find this stuff interesting.
Normal people (like you and me!) just have to grin and bear it. Oh, and _learn it_ as well, of course
— don't forget the small matter of those little Exams you've got coming up... remember?

Acids With Carbonates and Ammonia

More gripping reactions involving acids. At least there's some bubbles involved here.

Acid + Carbonate → Salt + Water + Carbon dioxide

1) *Definitely* learn the fact that acids with *carbonates* give off *carbon dioxide*.
2) If you also *practise* writing the following equations out *from memory*, it'll do you no harm at all.

hydrochloric acid + sodium carbonate → sodium chloride + water + carbon dioxide
$$2HCl + Na_2CO_3 \rightarrow 2NaCl + H_2O + CO_2$$

sulphuric acid + calcium carbonate → calcium sulphate + water + carbon dioxide
$$H_2SO_4 + CaCO_3 \rightarrow CaSO_4 + H_2O + CO_2$$

The Test For Carbon dioxide: It turns limewater milky

1) Bubble the gas through *limewater*.
2) If it's *carbon dioxide* the *limewater turns milky*.

Acid + Carbonate

CO_2 turning limewater milky

Dilute Acid + Ammonia → Ammonium salt

Learn that, then learn these three equations till you can write them out yourself, *from memory*:

Hydrochloric acid + Ammonia → Ammonium chloride
$$HCl_{(aq)} + NH_{3(aq)} \rightarrow NH_4Cl_{(aq)}$$

Sulphuric acid + Ammonia → Ammonium sulphate
$$H_2SO_{4(aq)} + 2NH_{3(aq)} \rightarrow (NH_4)_2SO_{4(aq)}$$

Nitric acid + Ammonia → Ammonium nitrate
$$HNO_{3(aq)} + NH_{3(aq)} \rightarrow NH_4NO_{3(aq)}$$

This last reaction with nitric acid produces the famous *ammonium nitrate* fertiliser, much appreciated for its *double dose* of essential nitrogen. (See P. 31.)

Still Awake, eh? — learning this page should finish you off...

Phew, the last page on acids, thank goodness. *Learn* the last of these dreary facts and try to *scribble it down*.   (If there's an Acid Appreciation Action Group, they're sure gonna be after me.)

SECTION FIVE — PERIODIC TRENDS

Metals

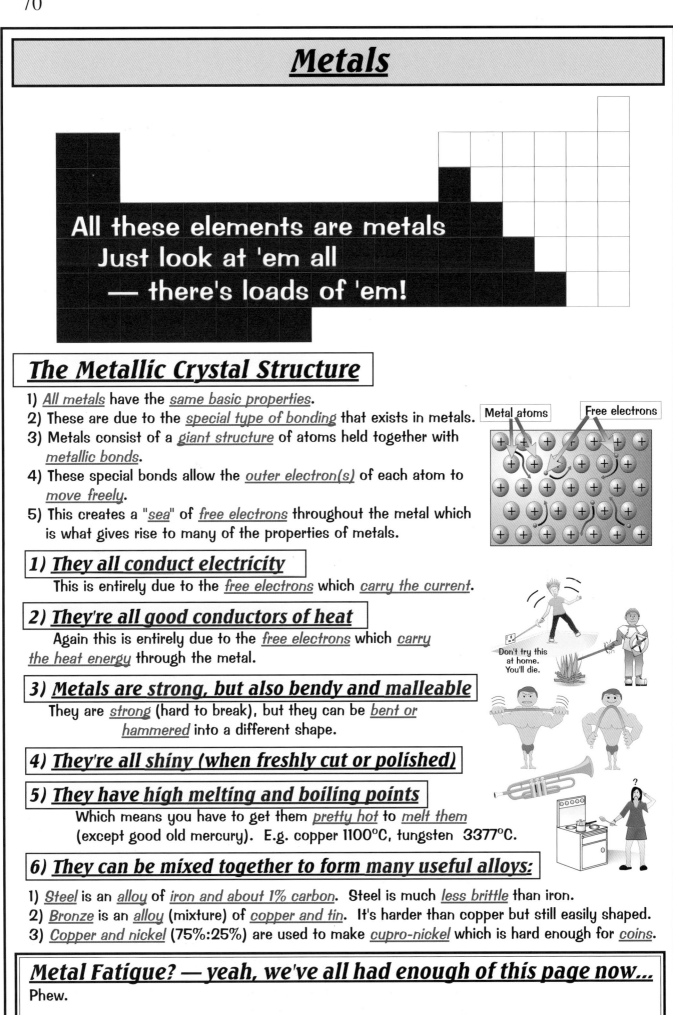

**All these elements are metals
Just look at 'em all
— there's loads of 'em!**

The Metallic Crystal Structure

1) _All metals_ have the _same basic properties_.
2) These are due to the _special type of bonding_ that exists in metals.
3) Metals consist of a _giant structure_ of atoms held together with _metallic bonds_.
4) These special bonds allow the _outer electron(s)_ of each atom to _move freely_.
5) This creates a "_sea_" of _free electrons_ throughout the metal which is what gives rise to many of the properties of metals.

Metal atoms   Free electrons

1) They all conduct electricity

This is entirely due to the _free electrons_ which _carry the current_.

2) They're all good conductors of heat

Again this is entirely due to the _free electrons_ which _carry the heat energy_ through the metal.

Don't try this at home. You'll die.

3) Metals are strong, but also bendy and malleable

They are _strong_ (hard to break), but they can be _bent or hammered_ into a different shape.

4) They're all shiny (when freshly cut or polished)

5) They have high melting and boiling points

Which means you have to get them _pretty hot_ to _melt them_ (except good old mercury). E.g. copper 1100°C, tungsten 3377°C.

6) They can be mixed together to form many useful alloys:

1) _Steel_ is an _alloy_ of _iron and about 1% carbon_. Steel is much _less brittle_ than iron.
2) _Bronze_ is an _alloy_ (mixture) of _copper and tin_. It's harder than copper but still easily shaped.
3) _Copper and nickel_ (75%:25%) are used to make _cupro-nickel_ which is hard enough for _coins_.

Metal Fatigue? — yeah, we've all had enough of this page now...

Phew.

Non-Metals

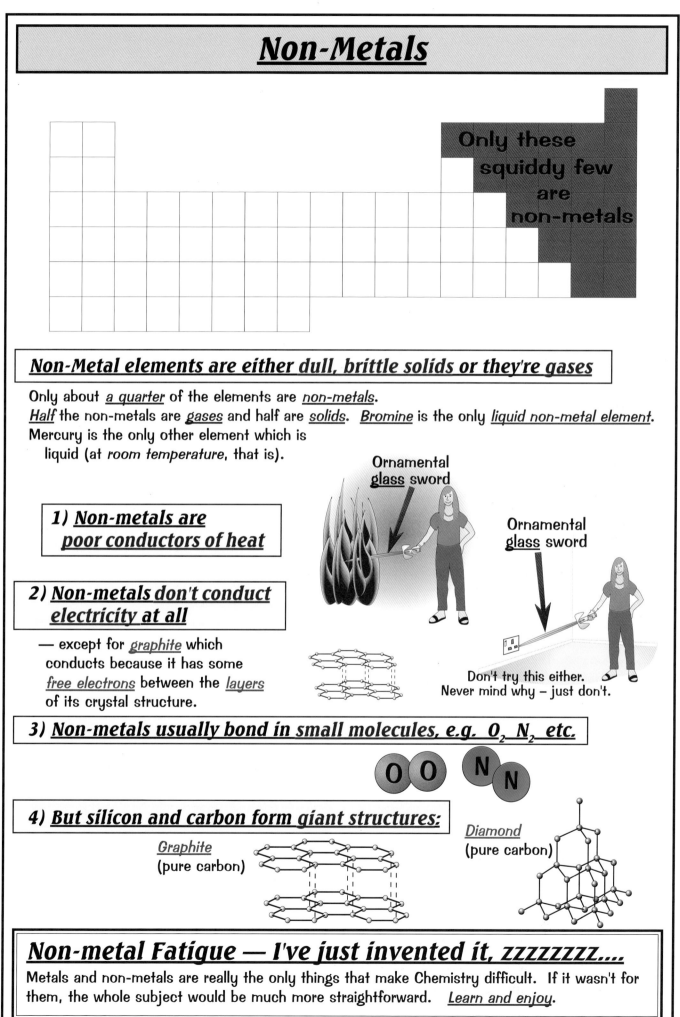

Only these squiddy few are non-metals

Non-Metal elements are either dull, brittle solids or they're gases

Only about _a quarter_ of the elements are _non-metals_.
Half the non-metals are _gases_ and half are _solids_. _Bromine_ is the only _liquid non-metal element_.
Mercury is the only other element which is liquid (at _room temperature_, that is).

Ornamental glass sword

1) Non-metals are poor conductors of heat

2) Non-metals don't conduct electricity at all

— except for _graphite_ which conducts because it has some _free electrons_ between the _layers_ of its crystal structure.

Ornamental glass sword

Don't try this either. Never mind why — just don't.

3) Non-metals usually bond in small molecules, e.g. O_2 N_2 etc.

O O   N N

4) But silicon and carbon form giant structures:

Graphite (pure carbon)

Diamond (pure carbon)

Non-metal Fatigue — I've just invented it, zzzzzzzz....

Metals and non-metals are really the only things that make Chemistry difficult. If it wasn't for them, the whole subject would be much more straightforward. _Learn and enjoy_.

The Reactivity Series of Metals

You must learn this Reactivity Series

You really should know which are the more reactive metals and which are the less reactive ones.

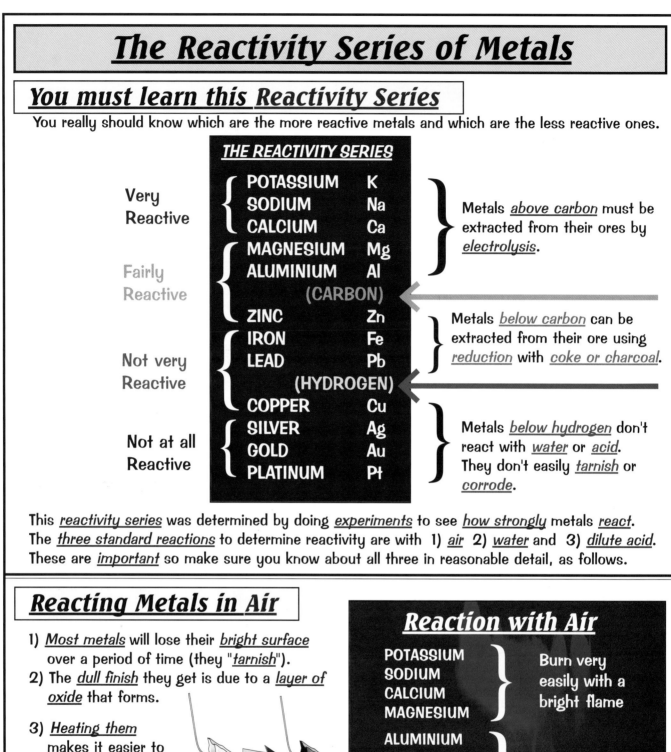

THE REACTIVITY SERIES

Very Reactive
- POTASSIUM   K
- SODIUM   Na
- CALCIUM   Ca

Fairly Reactive
- MAGNESIUM   Mg
- ALUMINIUM   Al
- (CARBON)

Not very Reactive
- ZINC   Zn
- IRON   Fe
- LEAD   Pb
- (HYDROGEN)
- COPPER   Cu

Not at all Reactive
- SILVER   Ag
- GOLD   Au
- PLATINUM   Pt

Metals *above carbon* must be extracted from their ores by *electrolysis*.

Metals *below carbon* can be extracted from their ore using *reduction* with *coke or charcoal*.

Metals *below hydrogen* don't react with *water* or *acid*. They don't easily *tarnish* or *corrode*.

This *reactivity series* was determined by doing *experiments* to see *how strongly* metals *react*. The *three standard reactions* to determine reactivity are with 1) *air* 2) *water* and 3) *dilute acid*. These are *important* so make sure you know about all three in reasonable detail, as follows.

Reacting Metals in Air

1) *Most metals* will lose their *bright surface* over a period of time (they "*tarnish*").
2) The *dull finish* they get is due to a *layer of oxide* that forms.

3) *Heating them* makes it easier to see how *reactive* they are, compared to each other.

layer of oxide

4) The equation is *real simple*:

Metal + Oxygen → Metal Oxide

Reaction with Air

- POTASSIUM
- SODIUM
- CALCIUM
- MAGNESIUM

Burn very easily with a bright flame

- ALUMINIUM
- ZINC
- IRON
- LEAD
- COPPER

React slowly with air when heated

- SILVER
- GOLD

No reaction

Examples: 1) $2Fe + O_2 \rightarrow 2FeO$ 2) $4Na + O_2 \rightarrow 2Na_2O$

How to get a good reaction — just smile ... ☺

Believe it or not they could easily give you a question asking what happens when copper is heated in air, and when calcium is heated in air. That means *all these details need learning*.

SECTION FIVE — PERIODIC TRENDS

Reactivity of Metals

Reacting Metals With Water

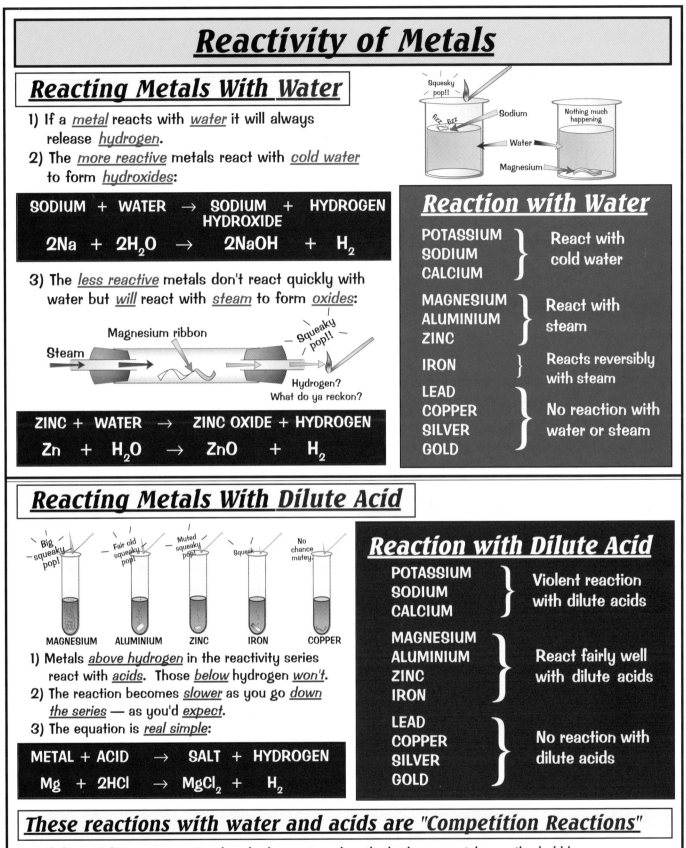

1) If a _metal_ reacts with _water_ it will always release _hydrogen_.
2) The _more reactive_ metals react with _cold water_ to form _hydroxides_:

SODIUM + WATER → SODIUM + HYDROGEN
HYDROXIDE

$$2Na + 2H_2O \rightarrow 2NaOH + H_2$$

3) The _less reactive_ metals don't react quickly with water but _will_ react with _steam_ to form _oxides_:

ZINC + WATER → ZINC OXIDE + HYDROGEN

$$Zn + H_2O \rightarrow ZnO + H_2$$

Reaction with Water

POTASSIUM SODIUM CALCIUM	React with cold water
MAGNESIUM ALUMINIUM ZINC	React with steam
IRON	Reacts reversibly with steam
LEAD COPPER SILVER GOLD	No reaction with water or steam

Reacting Metals With Dilute Acid

1) Metals _above hydrogen_ in the reactivity series react with _acids_. Those _below_ hydrogen _won't_.
2) The reaction becomes _slower_ as you go _down the series_ — as you'd _expect_.
3) The equation is _real simple_:

METAL + ACID → SALT + HYDROGEN

$$Mg + 2HCl \rightarrow MgCl_2 + H_2$$

Reaction with Dilute Acid

POTASSIUM SODIUM CALCIUM	Violent reaction with dilute acids
MAGNESIUM ALUMINIUM ZINC IRON	React fairly well with dilute acids
LEAD COPPER SILVER GOLD	No reaction with dilute acids

These reactions with water and acids are "Competition Reactions"

1) If the metal is _more reactive_ than _hydrogen_ it pushes the hydrogen _out_, hence the _bubbles_.
2) The metal _replaces_ the hydrogen in the compound. E.g. in water, the metal "steals" the oxygen from the hydrogen to form a _metal oxide_. The _hydrogen_ is then released as _gas bubbles_.
3) If the metal is _less reactive_ than hydrogen, then it _won't_ be able to displace it and _nothing will happen_.

All this just to say "some metals react more than others"...

I must say there's quite a lot of tricky details in these two pages. It's tempting to say that they can't possibly expect you to know them all. But then you look at the Exam questions and there they are, asking you precisely these kind of tricky details. Tough toffee, pal. _Learn and enjoy._

Metal Displacement Reactions

There's only one _golden rule_ here:

> ## A _MORE_ reactive metal will _displace_ a _LESS_ reactive metal from a compound

1) This is such a simple idea, surely.
2) You know all about the reactivity series — _some metals react more strongly than others_.
3) So if you put a _reactive_ metal like magnesium in a chemical solution you'd expect it to react.
4) If the chemical solution is a _dissolved metal compound_, then the _reactive_ metal that you add will _replace_ the _less reactive_ metal in the compound.
5) The metal that's "_kicked out_" will then appear as _fresh metal_ somewhere in the solution.
6) But if the metal added is _less reactive_ than the one in solution, then _no reaction_ will take place.

The Virtually World Famous Iron Nail in Copper Sulphate demo

A _MORE_ REACTIVE METAL WILL _DISPLACE_ A _LESS_ REACTIVE METAL:

1) Put an _iron nail_ in a solution of _copper(II) sulphate_ and you'll see _two_ things happen:

> a) The iron nail will become _coated with copper_.
> b) The _blue_ solution will turn _colourless_.

2) This is because the _iron_ is _more reactive_ than the copper and _displaces_ it from the solution.
3) This produces _fresh copper metal_ on the nail and a _colourless_ solution of _iron sulphate_.

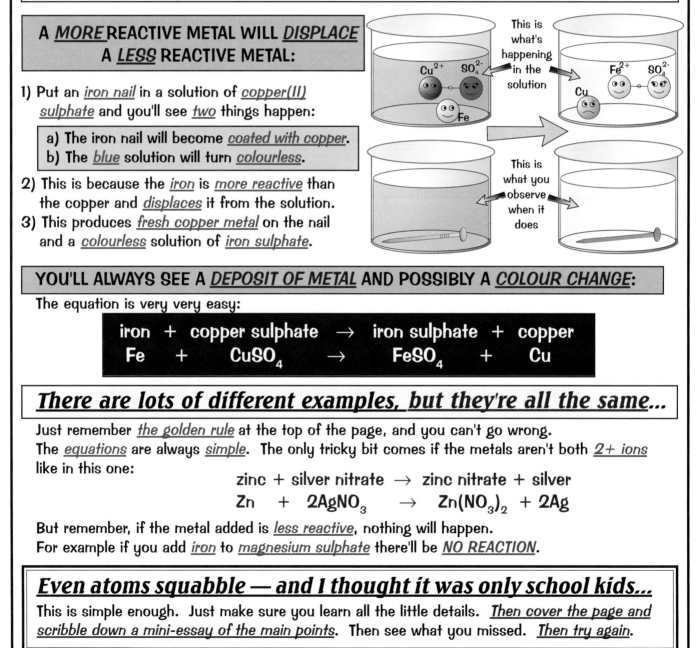

YOU'LL ALWAYS SEE A _DEPOSIT OF METAL_ AND POSSIBLY A _COLOUR CHANGE_:

The equation is very very easy:

> iron + copper sulphate → iron sulphate + copper
> Fe + $CuSO_4$ → $FeSO_4$ + Cu

There are lots of different examples, but they're all the same...

Just remember _the golden rule_ at the top of the page, and you can't go wrong.
The _equations_ are always _simple_. The only tricky bit comes if the metals aren't both _2+ ions_ like in this one:

> zinc + silver nitrate → zinc nitrate + silver
> Zn + $2AgNO_3$ → $Zn(NO_3)_2$ + $2Ag$

But remember, if the metal added is _less reactive_, nothing will happen.
For example if you add _iron_ to _magnesium sulphate_ there'll be _NO REACTION_.

Even atoms squabble — and I thought it was only school kids...

This is simple enough. Just make sure you learn all the little details. _Then cover the page and scribble down a mini-essay of the main points_. Then see what you missed. _Then try again._

Corrosion of Metals

Reactive metals will form _oxides_ quite _quickly_ when _exposed to the air_.
Most metals (e.g. aluminium) form quite decent _hard oxides_ that form a good _protective layer_.

But _iron_, woe of woes, does _no such thing_.
No, iron has to form the most appalling _red flaky oxide_ imaginable — the metal we use the _most_ just had to be the one that turns to _horrible useless rust_.
When God invented all the elements I bet he had a good old cackle to himself over that one.

The Rusting of Iron requires _both_ Air and Water

The _classic experiment_ on rust is to put _iron nails_ in various test tubes to see _how quickly_ they rust.

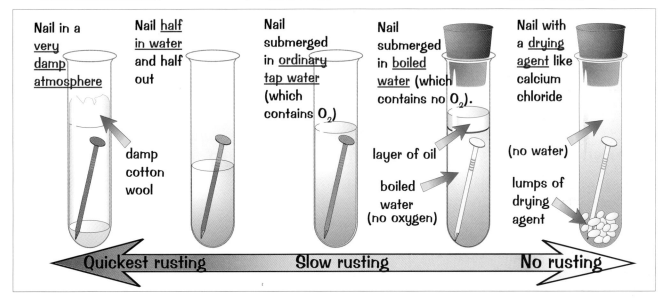

Nail in a very _damp_ atmosphere — damp cotton wool

Nail _half in water_ and half out

Nail submerged in _ordinary tap water_ (which contains O_2)

Nail submerged in _boiled water_ (which contains no O_2). — layer of oil — boiled water (no oxygen)

Nail with a _drying agent_ like calcium chloride — (no water) — lumps of drying agent

Quickest rusting ← Slow rusting → No rusting

The _rusting is quickest_ where there is most _air and water_ reaching the iron nail.
If _either_ air or water is _totally absent_ there'll be _no rusting at all_.

Rust is prevented by paint, oil or galvanising

1) _Painting_ is OK but where the _paint surface_ gets _damaged_, rust will get a grip and _spread_.
2) A coating of _oil or grease_ is better on bits of _moving machinery_ or on tools.
   However the oil has to be _constantly re-applied_ because it soon wears or washes off.

Galvanising gives great protection _even when damaged_

1) _Galvanising_ is the _best solution_ to rust prevention but it's more expensive.
   Galvanising is a process that _bonds a layer of zinc metal_ onto the surface of the _steel_.
2) The _big advantage_ with galvanisation is that even if the zinc coating gets _scratched_ or _damaged_, the exposed steel will _still not rust!_

Rust! Yeah, very funny, ho ho ho — but what about my little MGB...

At last! A page that has some relevance to everyday life. Who said you never learn anything useful at school. Not too much to learn here either. Try a couple of _mini-essays_ and make sure you can draw all those pretty test tubes too. _Then check back and see what you missed._

Transition Metals

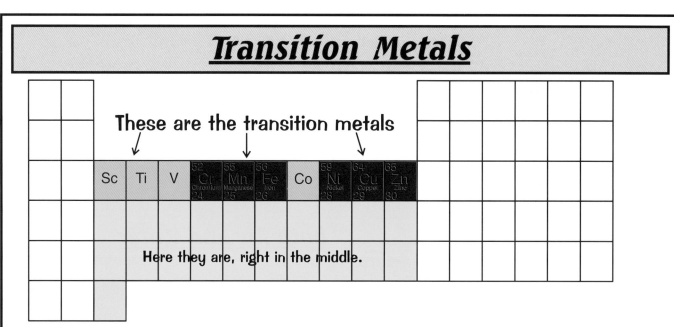

These are the transition metals

Here they are, right in the middle.

Chromium, Manganese, Iron, Nickel, Copper, Zinc

You need to know the ones shown above in red fairly well. You needn't worry about the others.

Transition Metals all have high melting point and high density

They're _typical metals_. They have the properties you would expect of a proper metal:
1) _Good conductors_ of heat and electricity.
2) Very _dense_, _strong_ and _shiny_.
3) Iron melts at 1500°C, copper melts at 1100°C and zinc melts at 400°C.

Transition Metals and their compounds all make good catalysts

1) _Iron_ is the _catalyst_ used in the _Haber process_ for making _ammonia_.
2) _Manganese(IV) oxide_ is a good _catalyst_ for the decomposition of _hydrogen peroxide_.
3) _Nickel_ is useful turning _oils into fats_ for making margarine.

The compounds are very colourful

1) The _compounds_ are _colourful_ due to the _transition metal ion_ they contain. e.g. _Potassium chromate(VI) is yellow_. _Potassium manganate(VII) is purple_. _Copper(II) sulphate is blue_.
2) The colour of people's _hair_ and also the colours in _gemstones_ like _blue sapphires_ and _green emeralds_ are all due to _transition metals_.

Uses of Iron, Copper and Zinc

1) _Iron_ is used for _man-hole covers_. _Pure iron is very brittle_, unlike steel which is more useful.
2) _Copper_ is used for _electric wiring_ and household _water pipes_. Copper and _nickel_ make _coins_.
3) _Zinc_ is used for _galvanising_ iron. _Zinc and copper_ make the alloy _brass_ for trumpets and tubas.

Lots of pretty colours — that's what we like to see...

There's quite a few things to learn about transition metals. First try to remember the five headings. Then learn the details that go under each one. _Keep trying to scribble it all down_.

Revision Summary for Section Five

Phew, I tell you what you know — there's some serious Chemistry in Section Five.
I suppose it makes up for Section Four being so easy. This is where all the really grisly stuff is.
All I can say is, just keep trying to learn it. These jolly questions will give you some idea of how
well you're doing. For any you can't do, you'll find the answers somewhere in Section Five.

1) What two properties did they base the early periodic table on?
2) Who was the old rogue who had the best shot at it and why was his table so clever?
3) What feature of atoms determines the order of the modern Periodic Table?
4) What are the Periods and Groups?
5) Explain the significance of "Periods" and "Groups" in terms of electron shells.
6) Draw diagrams to show the electron arrangements for the first twenty elements.
7) What are the electron arrangements of the noble gases? What are the properties of them?
8) Give two uses each for helium, neon and argon.
9) Which Group are the alkali metals? What is their outer shell like?
10) List four physical properties, and two chemical properties of the alkali metals.
11) Give details of the reactions of the alkali metals with water and chlorine, and burning in air.
12) What can you say about the pH of alkali metal oxides and hydroxides?
13) Describe the trends in appearance and reactivity of the halogens as you go down the Group.
14) List four properties common to all the halogens.
15) Give details, with equations, of the reaction of the halogens with metals, including silver.
16) Give details, with equations, of the displacement reactions of the halogens.
17) What is hydrogen chloride? Exactly how do you produce an acid from it?
18) What are the two sources of salt and what are the three main uses of it?
19) Draw a full diagram of a diaphragm cell and list the three useful products it creates.
20) Give a use for each of the four halogens: fluorine, chlorine, bromine and iodine.
21) Give uses for the three products from the electrolysis of brine.
22) Describe fully the colour of universal indicator for every pH value from 1 to 14.
23) What is neutralisation?
24) What is the equation for reacting acid with metal? Which metal(s) don't react with acid?
25) What type of salts do hydrochloric acid and sulphuric acid produce?
26) What type of reaction is "acid + metal oxide", or "acid + metal hydroxide"?
27) What about the oxides of non-metals — are they acidic or alkaline?
28) What is the equation for reacting acids with carbonates?
29) What is the equation for reacting dilute acid with ammonia?
30) What proportion of the elements are metals? What do all metals contain?
31) List six properties of metals. List four properties of non-metals.
32) Write down the twelve common metals in the order of the Reactivity Series.
33) Where do carbon and hydrogen fit in and what is the significance of their positions?
34) Describe the reaction of all twelve metals when heated in air. (Yes, *twelve*)
35) Describe the reaction of all twelve metals with water (or steam).
36) Describe the reaction of all twelve metals with dilute acid.
37) Explain fully what happens when you put an iron nail in copper sulphate solution.
38) What type of reaction is this? Give two other examples, with equations.
39) What is "special" about iron(III) oxide compared to other metal oxides?
40) Draw the five test tubes for the classic rusty nail experiment and say what happens.
41) Why is galvanising so good, compared to painting?
42) List three properties of transition metals, and two properties of their compounds.
43) Name six transition metals, and give uses for three of them.

Rates of Reaction

Reactions can go at all sorts of different rates

1) One of the _slowest_ is the _rusting_ of iron (it's not slow enough though — what about my little MGB).
2) A _moderate speed_ reaction is a _metal_ (like magnesium) reacting with _acid_ to produce a _gentle stream of bubbles_.
3) A _really fast_ reaction is an _explosion_, where it's all over in a _fraction of a second_.

Three ways to Measure the Speed of a Reaction

The _speed of reaction_ can be observed _either_ by how quickly the _reactants are used up_ or how quickly the _products are forming_. It's usually a lot easier to measure _products forming_. There are _three different ways_ that the speed of a reaction can be _measured_:

1) Precipitation

This is when the _product_ of the reaction is a _precipitate_ which _clouds the solution_. Observe a _marker_ through the solution and measure _how long it takes_ for it to _disappear_.

2) Change in mass (usually gas given off)

Any reaction that _produces a gas_ can be carried out on a _mass balance_ and as the gas is released the mass _disappearing_ is easily measured.

3) The volume of gas given off

This involves the use of a _gas syringe_ to measure the volume of gas given off. But that's about all there is to it.

The Rate of a Reaction Depends on Four Things:

1) _TEMPERATURE_
2) _CONCENTRATION_ — (or _PRESSURE_ for gases)
3) _SIZE OF PARTICLES_ — (or _SURFACE AREA_)
4) _CATALYST_

LEARN THEM!

Typical Graphs for Rate of Reaction

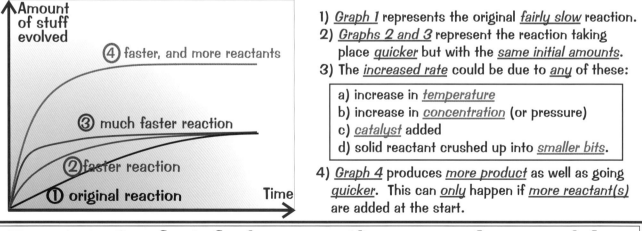

1) _Graph 1_ represents the original _fairly slow_ reaction.
2) _Graphs 2 and 3_ represent the reaction taking place _quicker_ but with the _same initial amounts_.
3) The _increased rate_ could be due to _any_ of these:
   a) increase in _temperature_
   b) increase in _concentration_ (or pressure)
   c) _catalyst_ added
   d) solid reactant crushed up into _smaller bits_.
4) _Graph 4_ produces _more product_ as well as going _quicker_. This can _only_ happen if _more reactant(s)_ are added at the start.

How to get a fast, furious reaction — crack a wee joke...

There's all sorts of bits and bobs of information on this page. To learn it all, you've got to learn to split it up into separate sections and do them one at a time. Practise by _covering the page_ and seeing how much you can _scribble down_ for each section. _Then try again, and again..._

Collision Theory

Reaction rates are explained perfectly by *Collision Theory*. It's really simple. It just says that *the rate of a reaction* simply depends on *how often* and *how hard* the reacting particles *collide* with each other. The basic idea is that particles have to *collide* in order to *react*, and they have to collide *hard enough* as well.

More Collisions increases the Rate of Reaction

All *four* methods of increasing the *rate of reaction* can be *explained* in terms of increasing the *number of collisions* between the reacting particles.

1) TEMPERATURE increases the no. of collisions

When the *temperature is increased* the particles all *move quicker*. If they're moving quicker, they're going to have *more collisions*.

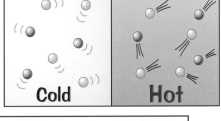
Cold   Hot

2) CONCENTRATION (or PRESSURE) increases the number of collisions

If the solution is made more *concentrated* it means there are more particles of *reactant* knocking about *between the water molecules* which makes collisions between the *important* particles *more likely*. In a *gas*, increasing the *pressure* means the molecules are *more squashed up* together so there are going to be *more collisions*.

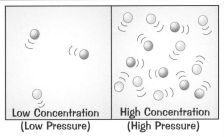
Low Concentration (Low Pressure)   High Concentration (High Pressure)

3) SIZE OF SOLID PARTICLES (or SURFACE AREA) increases collisions

If one of the reactants is a *solid* then *breaking it up* into *smaller* pieces will *increase its surface area*. This means the particles around it in the solution will have *more area to work on* so there'll be *more useful collisions*.

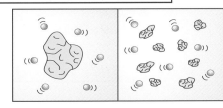

Faster Collisions increase the Rate of Reaction

Higher temperature also increases the *energy* of the collisions, because it makes all the particles *move faster*.

Faster collisions are ONLY caused by increasing the temperature

Reactions *only happen* if the particles collide with *enough energy*.

At a *higher temperature* there will be *more particles* colliding with *enough energy* to make the reaction happen.

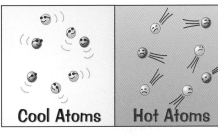
Cool Atoms   Hot Atoms

Collision Theory — I reckon it's always women drivers...

This is quite easy I think. Isn't it all kind of obvious — at least once you've been told it, anyway. The more often particles collide and the harder they hit, the greater the reaction rate. There's a few extra picky details of course (isn't there always!), *but you've only got to LEARN them...*

80

Four Experiments on Rate of Reaction

REMEMBER: Any reaction can be used to investigate any of the four factors that affect the rate. These pages illustrate four important reactions, but only one factor has been considered for each. But we could just as easily use, say, the marble chips/acid reaction to test the effect of temperature instead.

1) Reaction of Hydrochloric Acid and Marble Chips

This experiment is often used to demonstrate the effect of breaking the solid up into small bits.

1) Measure the volume of gas evolved with a gas syringe and take readings at regular intervals.
2) Make a table of readings and plot them as a graph.
3) Repeat the experiment with exactly the same volume of acid, and exactly the same mass of marble chips, but with the marble more crunched up.
4) Then repeat with the same mass of powdered chalk instead of marble chips.

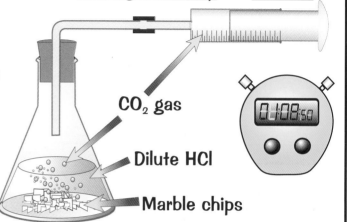

CO₂ gas

Dilute HCl

Marble chips

These graphs show the effect of using finer particles of solid

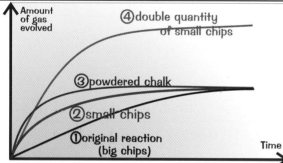

1) The increase in surface area causes more collisions so the rate of reaction is faster.
2) Graph 4 shows the reaction if a greater mass of small marble chips is added.
3) The extra surface area gives a quicker reaction and there is also more gas evolved overall.

2) Reaction of Magnesium Metal With Dilute HCl

1) This reaction is good for measuring the effects of increased concentration, (as is the marble/acid reaction).
2) This reaction gives off hydrogen gas, which we can measure with a mass balance, as shown. (The other method is to use a gas syringe, as above.)

These graphs show the effect of using stronger acid solutions

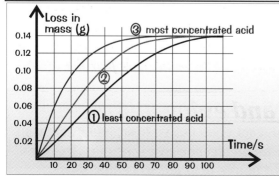

1) Take readings of mass at regular time intervals.
2) Put the results in a table and work out the loss in mass for each reading. Plot a graph.
3) Repeat with stronger acid solutions but always with the same amount of magnesium.
4) The volume of acid must always be kept the same too — only the concentration is increased.
5) The three graphs show the same old pattern. Higher concentration giving a steeper graph with the reaction finishing much quicker.

SECTION SIX — REACTION RATES

Four Experiments on Rate of Reaction

3) Sodium Thiosulphate and HCl produce a Cloudy Precipitate

1) These two chemicals are both _clear solutions_.
2) They react together to form a _yellow precipitate_ of _sulphur_.
3) _The experiment_ involves watching a black mark _disappear_ through the _cloudy sulphur_ and _timing_ how long it takes to go.

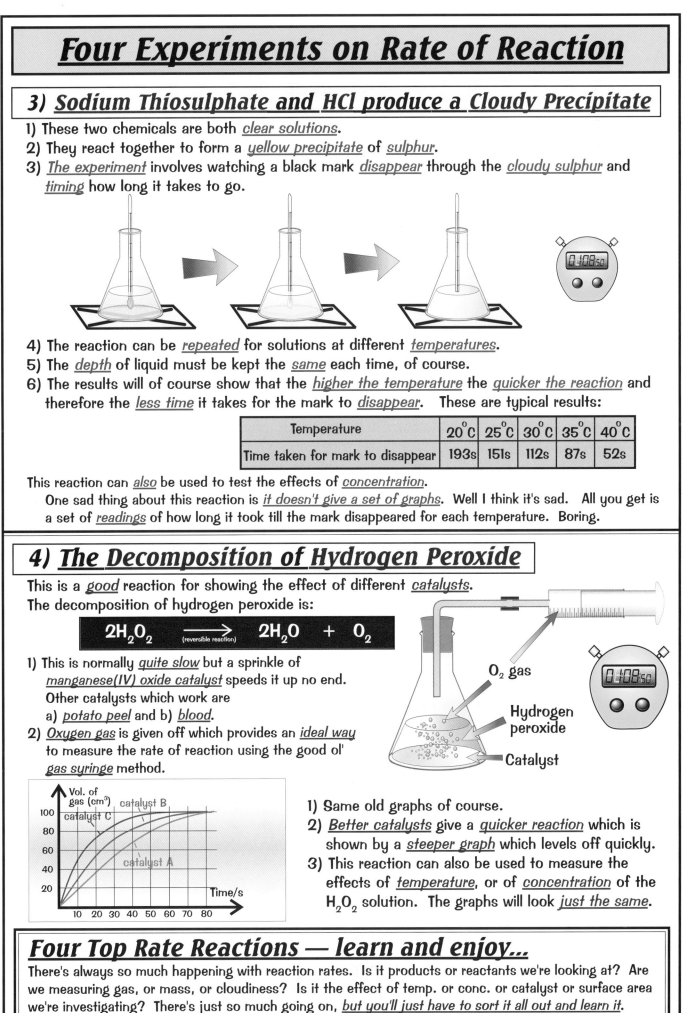

4) The reaction can be _repeated_ for solutions at different _temperatures_.
5) The _depth_ of liquid must be kept the _same_ each time, of course.
6) The results will of course show that the _higher the temperature_ the _quicker the reaction_ and therefore the _less time_ it takes for the mark to _disappear_.   These are typical results:

Temperature	$20^{\circ}C$	$25^{\circ}C$	$30^{\circ}C$	$35^{\circ}C$	$40^{\circ}C$
Time taken for mark to disappear	193s	151s	112s	87s	52s

This reaction can _also_ be used to test the effects of _concentration_.
   One sad thing about this reaction is _it doesn't give a set of graphs_. Well I think it's sad.   All you get is a set of _readings_ of how long it took till the mark disappeared for each temperature. Boring.

4) The Decomposition of Hydrogen Peroxide

This is a _good_ reaction for showing the effect of different _catalysts_.
The decomposition of hydrogen peroxide is:

$$2H_2O_2 \xrightarrow{\text{(reversible reaction)}} 2H_2O + O_2$$

1) This is normally _quite slow_ but a sprinkle of _manganese(IV) oxide catalyst_ speeds it up no end. Other catalysts which work are
a) _potato peel_ and b) _blood_.
2) _Oxygen gas_ is given off which provides an _ideal way_ to measure the rate of reaction using the good ol' _gas syringe_ method.

O_2 gas

Hydrogen peroxide

Catalyst

1) Same old graphs of course.
2) _Better catalysts_ give a _quicker reaction_ which is shown by a _steeper graph_ which levels off quickly.
3) This reaction can also be used to measure the effects of _temperature_, or of _concentration_ of the H_2O_2 solution. The graphs will look _just the same_.

Four Top Rate Reactions — learn and enjoy...

There's always so much happening with reaction rates. Is it products or reactants we're looking at? Are we measuring gas, or mass, or cloudiness? Is it the effect of temp. or conc. or catalyst or surface area we're investigating? There's just so much going on, _but you'll just have to sort it all out and learn it_.

Catalysts

Many reactions can be _speeded up_ by adding a _catalyst_.

A _CATALYST_ is a substance which _INCREASES_ the speed of a reaction, without being _CHANGED_ or _USED UP_ in the reaction.

1) Catalysts work best when they have a Big Surface Area

1) Catalysts are usually used as a _powder_ or _pellets_ or a _fine gauze_.
2) This gives them _maximum surface area_ to enable the reacting particles to _meet up_ and do the business.

Catalyst Powder   Catalyst Pellets   Catalyst Gauzes

2) Catalysts Help Reduce Costs in Industrial Reactions

1) _Catalysts_ increase the rate of many _industrial reactions_, which saves a lot of _money_ simply because the plant doesn't need to operate for _as long_ to produce the _same amount_ of stuff.
2) Alternatively, a catalyst will allow the reaction to work at a _much lower temperature_ and that can save a lot of money too. Catalysts are therefore _very important_ for _commercial reasons_.
3) Catalysts are used _over and over again_. They may need _cleaning_ but they _don't_ get _used up_.

3) Transition metals are common catalysts

1) Transition metals are used as catalysts in many _industrial_ reactions.
2) Different _reactions_ use different _catalysts_. Make sure you _know these two_:

a) An Iron Catalyst is used in the Haber Process   (See P. 30)

$$N_{2\,(g)} \; + \; 3H_{2\,(g)} \xrightarrow[\text{reversible reaction}]{\text{Iron Catalyst}} 2NH_{3\,(g)}$$

b) A Platinum Catalyst is used in the production of Nitric Acid   (See P. 31)

$$\text{Ammonia} \; + \; \text{Oxygen} \xrightarrow{\text{Platinum Catalyst}} \text{Nitrogen monoxide} \; + \; \text{Water}$$

4) Catalytic Converters in Cars contain Platinum

1) These are fitted in the _exhaust system_ of all new cars.
2) Normal exhaust gases include _unburnt petrol_, _carbon monoxide_ and _oxides of nitrogen_.
3) The _catalytic converters_ cause a _reaction_ between these badly _polluting_ exhaust gases to produces _harmless gases_: — _nitrogen_, _oxygen_, _carbon dioxide_ and _water vapour_.

Catalysts are like great jokes — you can use them over and over...

Make sure you _learn the definition_ in the top box _word for word_.
The fact is they can easily ask you: _"What is a catalyst?" (2 Marks)._
This is much easier to answer if you have a "word for word" definition at the ready.
If you don't, you're likely to lose half the marks on it. That's a fact.

Biological Catalysts — Enzymes

Enzymes are Catalysts produced by Living Things

1) _Living things_ have thousands of different _chemical processes_ going on inside them.
2) The _quicker_ these happen the _better_, and raising the _temperature_ of the body is an important way to _speed them up_.
3) However, there's a _limit_ to how far you can _raise_ the temperature before _cells_ start getting _damaged_, so living things also produce _enzymes_ which act as _catalysts_ to _speed up_ all these chemical reactions _without_ the need for _high temperatures_.
4) _Enzymes_ themselves only _perform well_ within a fairly _narrow range_ of temperature.
5) Every _different_ biological process has its _own enzyme_ designed especially for it.
6) For example the way an _apple_ turns brown when cut is caused by a _particular_ enzyme.
7) Man is now starting to use _biological catalysts_ more and more for his _own purposes_.
8) Enzymes have _many advantages_ over traditional _non-organic_ catalysts:
    a) There's a _huge variety_ of enzymes.
    b) They're _not scarce_ like many metal catalysts, e.g. platinum.
    c) They _work best at low temperatures_, which keeps costs down.
    d) They can be _carefully selected_ to do a _precise job_.
EXAMPLES: "biological" washing powders, _dishwasher_ powders, and in the _treatment of leather_.

Enzymes Like it Warm but Not Too Hot

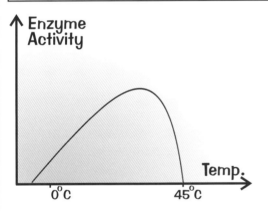

1) The _chemical reactions_ in _living cells_ are _quite fast_ in conditions that are _warm_ rather than _hot_.

2) This is because the cells use catalysts called _enzymes_, which are _protein molecules_.

3) Enzymes are usually _damaged_ by temperatures above about _45°C_, and as the graph shows, their activity _drops off sharply_ when the temperature gets _a little too high_.

Freezing food stops the enzyme activity (and the bacteria)

1) At _lower temperatures_, enzyme activity also _drops quite quickly_.
2) By _0°C_ there's virtually _nothing happening_.
3) This is the idea behind _refrigeration_, where foods are kept at about _4°C_ to keep _enzyme_ and _bacterial_ activity _to a minimum_ so that food stays _fresher_ for _longer_.
4) _Freezers_ store food at about _−20°C_ and at this temperature bacteria and enzymes _don't function at all_.
5) However, _they're not destroyed by freezing_ and once the food _thaws out_ they spring back into _action_. So frozen food should be _thawed carefully_ and then _cooked again_ before eating.
6) Cooking _destroys_ all bacteria and enzymes, so _properly cooked_ food is _safe to eat_.
7) However, even _cooked_ foods will go off _pretty rapidly_ if left in a _warm_ place.

"Enzymes" — sounds like a brand of throat lozenge...

This page is definitely a candidate for the mini-essay method. Two mini-essays in fact.
What else is there to say? _Scribble down the facts, then look back and see what you missed._

Uses of Enzymes

Living cells use chemical reactions to produce _new materials_. Many of these reactions provide products which are _useful_ to us. Here are _three_ important examples:

Yeast in Brewing of Beer and Wine: Fermentation

1) _Yeast cells_ convert _sugar_ into _carbon dioxide_ and _alcohol_.
2) They do this using the _enzyme_ ZYMASE.
3) The main thing is to _keep the temperature just right_.
4) If it's _too cold_ the enzyme won't work very _quickly_.
5) If it's _too hot_ it will _destroy_ the enzyme.
6) This biological process is called _fermentation_ and is used for making alcoholic drinks like _beer and wine_.

FERMENTATION is the process of _yeast_ converting _sugar_ into _carbon dioxide_ and _alcohol_.

$$Glucose \xrightarrow{\text{Zymase}} Carbon\ dioxide\ +\ Ethanol \quad (+ Energy)$$

Yeast in Bread-making: Fermentation again

1) The reaction in _bread-making_ is _exactly the same_ as that in _brewing_.
2) Yeast cells use the enzyme _zymase_ to break down sugar and this gives them _energy_.
3) It also releases carbon dioxide gas and alcohol as waste products.
4) The _carbon dioxide gas_ is produced _throughout_ the bread mixture and forms in _bubbles_ everywhere.
5) This makes the bread _rise_ and gives it it's familiar texture. The small amount of alcohol also gives the bread some extra flavour, no doubt.
6) When the bread is put in the _oven_ the yeast is _killed_ and the _reaction stops_.

Yoghurt and Cheese making — only pasteurised milk

1) _Pasteurised milk_ MUST be used for making _cheese_ and _yoghurt_, because _fresh_ milk contains many _unwanted bacteria_ which would give them a _bad taste_.
2) Instead the pasteurised milk is mixed with _specially grown cultures_ of bacteria.
3) This mixture is kept at the _ideal temperature_ for the bacteria and their enzymes to work.
4) For _yoghurt_ this is _pretty warm_ at about $45^{o}C$.
5) The _yoghurt-making bacteria_ convert _lactose_ (the natural sugar found in milk) into _lactic acid_. This gives yoghurts their slightly _bitter_ taste.
6) _Cheese_ on the other hand matures better in _cooler conditions_.
7) _Various_ bacterial enzymes can be used in _cheese making_ to produce different _textures_ and _tastes_.

With a face like that you could be Chief Curdler in a yoghurt factory, you could pal.

This page is just so easy— it's a blummin' picnic...

This is rapidly turning into a Domestic Science book. Anyway, you're expected to know all these details of making bread, wine, cheese and yoghurt. _Mini-essays again, I'd say._ Enjoy.

Simple Reversible Reactions

A _reversible reaction_ is one which can go _in both directions_.
In other words the _products_ of the reaction can be _turned back_ into the original _reactants_.
Here are some _examples_ you should know about in case they spring one on you in the Exam.

The Thermal decomposition of Ammonium Chloride

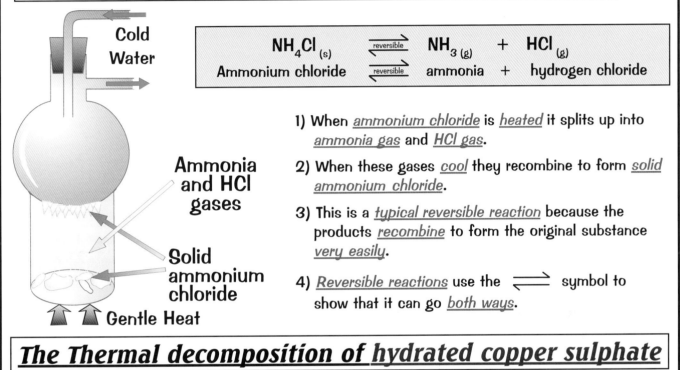

$$NH_4Cl_{(s)} \underset{reversible}{\overset{reversible}{\rightleftharpoons}} NH_{3(g)} + HCl_{(g)}$$
Ammonium chloride   ammonia   +   hydrogen chloride

Cold Water

Ammonia and HCl gases

Solid ammonium chloride

Gentle Heat

1) When _ammonium chloride_ is _heated_ it splits up into _ammonia gas_ and _HCl gas_.

2) When these gases _cool_ they recombine to form _solid ammonium chloride_.

3) This is a _typical reversible reaction_ because the products _recombine_ to form the original substance _very easily_.

4) _Reversible reactions_ use the $\rightleftharpoons$ symbol to show that it can go _both ways_.

The Thermal decomposition of hydrated copper sulphate

1) Good old dependable _blue copper(II) sulphate_ crystals here again.
2) Here they're displaying their usual trick, but under the guise of a _reversible reaction_.

3) If you _heat them_ it drives the water off and leaves _white anhydrous_ copper(II) sulphate powder.

4) If you then _add_ a couple of drops of _water_ to the _white powder_ you get the _blue crystals_ back again.

Water vapour

The proper name for the _blue crystals_ is _Hydrated copper(II) sulphate_.
"_Hydrated_" means "_with water_".
When you drive the water off they become a white powder, _Anhydrous copper(II) sulphate_.
"_Anhydrous_" means "_without water_".

Learn these simple reactions, then see what you know...

These are two nice simple examples of reversible reactions.
They could well come up in your Exam. There really isn't much to learn here. _Scribble it_.

Energy Transfer in Reactions

Whenever chemical reactions occur _energy_ is usually _transferred_ to or from the _surroundings_.

In an Exothermic Reaction, Heat is GIVEN OUT

An _EXOTHERMIC REACTION_ is one which _GIVES OUT ENERGY_ to the surroundings, usually in the form of _HEAT_ and usually shown by a _RISE IN TEMPERATURE_

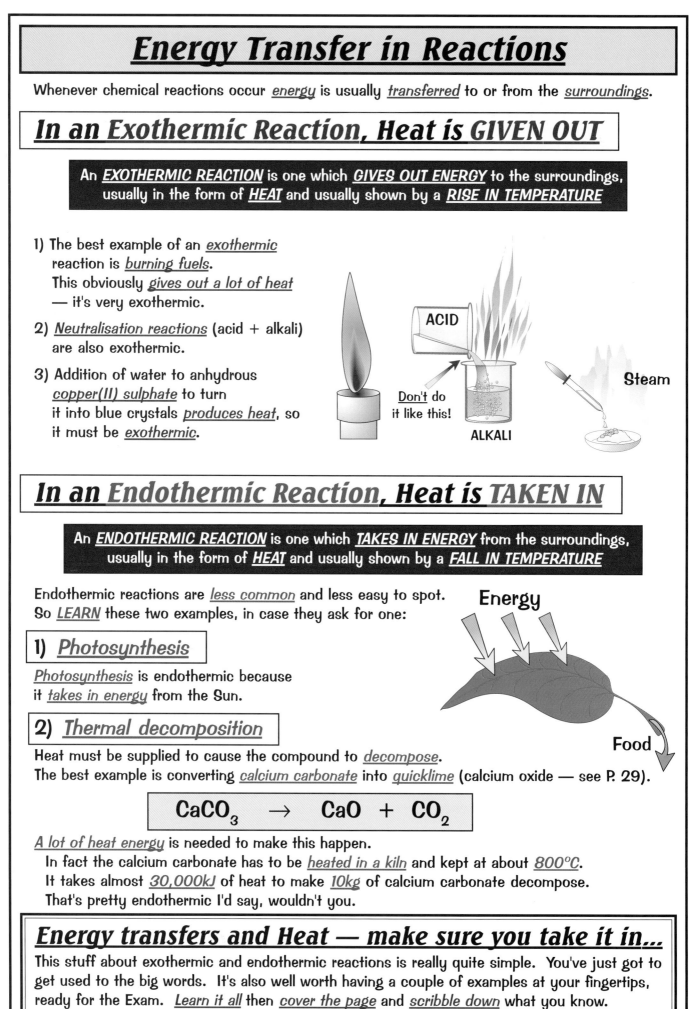

1) The best example of an _exothermic_ reaction is _burning fuels_. This obviously _gives out a lot of heat_ — it's very exothermic.

2) _Neutralisation reactions_ (acid + alkali) are also exothermic.

3) Addition of water to anhydrous _copper(II) sulphate_ to turn it into blue crystals _produces heat_, so it must be _exothermic_.

ACID

Don't do it like this!

ALKALI

Steam

In an Endothermic Reaction, Heat is TAKEN IN

An _ENDOTHERMIC REACTION_ is one which _TAKES IN ENERGY_ from the surroundings, usually in the form of _HEAT_ and usually shown by a _FALL IN TEMPERATURE_

Endothermic reactions are _less common_ and less easy to spot. So _LEARN_ these two examples, in case they ask for one:

Energy

1) Photosynthesis

Photosynthesis is endothermic because it _takes in energy_ from the Sun.

2) Thermal decomposition

Food

Heat must be supplied to cause the compound to _decompose_.
The best example is converting _calcium carbonate_ into _quicklime_ (calcium oxide — see P. 29).

$$CaCO_3 \rightarrow CaO + CO_2$$

A lot of heat energy is needed to make this happen.
In fact the calcium carbonate has to be _heated in a kiln_ and kept at about _800°C_.
It takes almost _30,000kJ_ of heat to make _10kg_ of calcium carbonate decompose.
That's pretty endothermic I'd say, wouldn't you.

Energy transfers and Heat — make sure you take it in...

This stuff about exothermic and endothermic reactions is really quite simple. You've just got to get used to the big words. It's also well worth having a couple of examples at your fingertips, ready for the Exam. _Learn it all_ then _cover the page_ and _scribble down_ what you know.

Energy Transfer in Reactions

Energy Must Always be Supplied to Break bonds...

During a chemical reaction, _old bonds are broken_ and _new bonds are formed_.

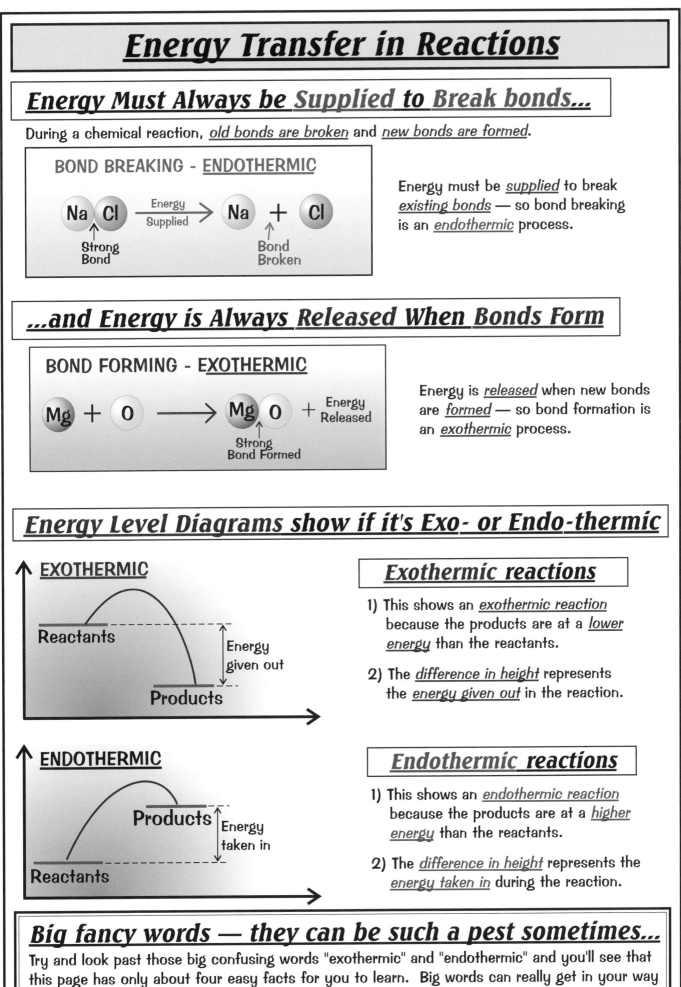

BOND BREAKING - ENDOTHERMIC

Na Cl → Na + Cl
Energy Supplied
Strong Bond
Bond Broken

Energy must be _supplied_ to break _existing bonds_ — so bond breaking is an _endothermic_ process.

...and Energy is Always Released When Bonds Form

BOND FORMING - EXOTHERMIC

Mg + O → MgO + Energy Released
Strong Bond Formed

Energy is _released_ when new bonds are _formed_ — so bond formation is an _exothermic_ process.

Energy Level Diagrams show if it's Exo- or Endo-thermic

EXOTHERMIC
Reactants
Products
Energy given out

Exothermic reactions

1) This shows an _exothermic reaction_ because the products are at a _lower energy_ than the reactants.

2) The _difference in height_ represents the _energy given out_ in the reaction.

ENDOTHERMIC
Products
Reactants
Energy taken in

Endothermic reactions

1) This shows an _endothermic reaction_ because the products are at a _higher energy_ than the reactants.

2) The _difference in height_ represents the _energy taken in_ during the reaction.

Big fancy words — they can be such a pest sometimes...

Try and look past those big confusing words "exothermic" and "endothermic" and you'll see that this page has only about four easy facts for you to learn. Big words can really get in your way sometimes if you let them get the better of you. Don't let them, _learn what they mean_ instead!

Revision Summary for Section Six

This section isn't too bad really. Well it's short for one thing. That always helps.
I suppose some of the stuff on Rates of Reaction gets a bit chewy in places, but the rest is all a
bit of a breeze really, isn't it? Anyway, here's some more of those nice easy questions which
you enjoy so much. Remember, if you can't answer one, look at the appropriate page and learn
it. Then go back and try them again. Your hope is that one day you'll be able to glide
effortlessly through all of them — it's a nice trick if you can do it.

1) What are the three different ways of measuring the speed of a reaction?
2) What are the four factors which the rate of reaction depends on?
3) Explain how each of these four factors increases the *number of collisions* between particles.
4) What is the other aspect of collision theory which determines the rate of reaction?
5) Which is the only physical factor which affects this other aspect of the collisions?
6) What happens when hydrochloric acid is added to marble chips?
7) Give details of the two possible methods for measuring the rate of this reaction.
8) Sketch a typical set of graphs for either of these methods.
9) Describe in detail how you would test the effect on the reaction rate of
    a) finer particles of solid   b) stronger concentration of acid   c) temperature.
10) What happens when sodium thiosulphate is added to HCl?   How is the rate measured?
11) Write down the equation for the decomposition of hydrogen peroxide.
12) What is the best way to increase the rate of this reaction?
13) What is the best way to measure the rate of this reaction? What will the graphs look like?
14) What is the definition of a catalyst?
15) Name two specific industrial catalysts and give the process that each is used in.
16) What are enzymes? Where are they made? Give three examples of their use by man.
17) Sketch the graph for enzyme activity vs temperature, indicating the temperatures.
18) What effect does freezing have on food? What happens when you thaw it out?
19) Give the word-equation for fermentation. Which organism and which enzyme are involved?
20) Explain what happens in brewing and bread-making.   What is the difference between them?
21) What kind of milk is needed for making cheese and yoghurt and why?
22) What gives yoghurt and cheese their flavour?
23) What is a reversible reaction?   Describe two simple reversible reactions in detail.
24) What is an exothermic reaction? What effect does it have on the surroundings?
25) What is an endothermic reaction? What effect does it have on the surroundings?
26) Give two examples of exothermic and two examples of endothermic reactions.
27) Draw energy level diagrams for these two types of reaction.
28) What energy transfers takes place when bonds are   i) broken   ii) formed?

Answers

P.34 *1)* $2HCl_{(aq)} + Ca_{(s)} \rightarrow CaCl_{2(aq)} + H_{2(g)}$ *2)* $2K_{(s)} + 2H_2O_{(l)} \rightarrow 2KOH_{(aq)} + H_{2(g)}$
    3) $2HCl_{(aq)} + Na_2O_{(s)} \rightarrow 2NaCl_{(aq)} + H_2O_{(l)}$ *4)* $CH_{4(g)} + 2O_{2(g)} \rightarrow CO_{2(g)} + 2H_2O_{(g)}$

P.36 *1)* Cu =64, K =39, Kr =84, Fe =56, Cl =35.5   *2)* NaOH =40, Fe_2O_3=160, C_6H_{14}=86, $Mg(NO_3)_2$=148

P.37 *1) a)* 30.0% *b)* 88.9% *c)* 48.0% *d)* 65.3%   *2) a)* 22.2% *b)* 30.4% *c)* 21.5% *d)* 19.7%

P.38 Revision Summary

20)   *a)* $2HCl_{(aq)} + MgO_{(s)} \rightarrow MgCl_{2(aq)} + H_2O_{(l)}$ *b)* $2HCl_{(aq)} + 2Na_{(s)} \rightarrow 2NaCl_{(aq)} + H_{2(g)}$
    c) $CaCO_{3(s)} + 2HCl_{(aq)} \rightarrow CaCl_{2(aq)} + H_2O_{(l)} + CO_{2(g)}$ *d)* $Ca_{(s)} + 2H_2O_{(l)} \rightarrow Ca(OH)_{2(aq)} + H_{2(g)}$
    e) $Fe_2O_{3(s)} + 3H_{2(g)} \rightarrow 2Fe_{(s)} + 3H_2O_{(g)}$ *f)* $C_3H_{8(g)} + 5O_{2(g)} \rightarrow 3CO_{2(g)} + 4H_2O_{(g)}$

26)   *a)* Ca =40 *b)* Ag =108 *c)* CO_2 =44 *d)* $MgCO_3$ =84 *e)* Na_2CO_3 =106 *f)* ZnO =81
    g) KOH =56 *h)* NH_3 =17 *i)* C_4H_{10} =58 j) NaCl =58.5 *k)* $FeCl_3$ =162.5

27)   *a)* 40.0% *b) i)* 12.0% *ii)* 27.3% *iii)* 75.0% *c) i)* 74.2% *ii)* 70.0% *iii)* 52.9%

Index

A

a nice trick if you can do it 88
ace 8, 18, 46, 56
acid rain 29, 42, 45, 66, 68
acid soils 29, 66
acidity in lakes 29
acids 31, 35, 45, 61, 63, 66,
    67, 69, 78
Africa 51
air 12, 30, 61
air molecules 4
airships 58
alcohol 84
alkalis 31, 60, 65, 66, 68
alkali metals 59-61
alkanes 20, 21
alkenes 21
alloys 28, 70
aluminium 12, 25, 26, 28, 29, 67,
    72, 73
aluminium chloride 63
aluminium ore 23
aluminium oxide 20, 23, 26
ammonia 5, 30, 31, 40, 69, 85
ammonium chloride 69, 85
ammonium nitrate fertiliser 31, 69
Andes 52
anions 10, 35
anode 25, 26, 35
answers 88
aqueous 34
A$_r$ (Relative Atomic Mass) 36, 37,
    55
argon 12, 39, 40, 58
Atlantic 53
atmosphere 39, 40, 41
atmospheric problems 42, 43
atomic mass 55
atomic number 7, 36, 55, 56
atoms 6-12, 34, 36, 57
attraction 9

B

bacteria 31, 83, 84
balancing equations 34
Barrow Town Hall 47, 48, 49
basalt 46, 49, 53
basic stuff 1, 11, 15
battery 35
bauxite 23, 26
beer and wine 84
big bubbles of gas 2
big scary names 36
biological catalysts 83
bitumen 18
blast furnace 24

bleach 15, 65
bloodcurdling 36
blue flame 19
boiling 2, 14
boiling points 10, 11, 19
boring brown bromine 5
bottled gas 18
bouncing 1
brass 28, 76
bread-making 84
breaking bonds 3
brewing 84
bright specks 4
brine 64, 65
bromine 5, 60, 62, 63, 65, 71
bronze 28, 70
Brownian motion 4
building 29
bumping 4
burning 42, 44, 61, 86
butane 21

C

caesium 59
calcium 8, 23, 72, 73
calcium carbonate 29, 36, 47
calcium chloride 75
calcium hydroxide 66
calcium oxide 24, 29
calcium silicate 24
carbon 11, 18, 23, 24, 25, 26,
    36, 41, 44, 72
carbon atoms 21
Carbon Cycle 44
carbon dioxide 12, 15, 19, 21,
    24, 39, 40, 43, 44, 68,
    69, 82, 84
carbon monoxide 19, 23, 24, 82
carbon tetrachloride 62
carbon-12 and carbon-14 7
carbonates 69
carbonic acid 68
cars 42
catalysts 20, 22, 30, 33, 76, 78,
    81-83
catalytic converters 82
cathode 25, 27, 35
cations 10, 35
cement 29
CFC gases 42
chalk 44, 80
changes of state 2
charged particles 6, 9
chat-up lines 28, 33
cheese 84
chemical behaviour 7

chemical bonds 10
chemical energy 17
chip butties 61
chlorine 8, 9, 10, 15, 60-65
chromatography 13
chromium 76
clay 29, 48
clean blue flame. 19
climate 43
clouds 42, 45
cloudy precipitate 81
coal 17, 44
cobalt chloride paper 15
coke 24, 72
cold! 58
collide 1
collision theory 79
coloured flames 61
combustion 19
competition reactions 73
compounds 12, 13, 23, 36, 37
compressed 1, 48
compression 46
concentration 78-81
concrete 29
condense 14, 18, 30, 45
conduct electricity 10, 28, 35, 70
conductors of heat 28, 70
confused haze 33
conglomerates 47
continental drift 53
continental plates 50-52
cooling graphs 3
copper 12, 25, 28, 39,
    67, 70, 72-74, 76
copper ore 23
copper oxide 39
copper sulphate 15, 74, 85, 86
copper(II) carbonate 23
core 50
corrosion 28, 72, 75
corrosive 15
costs 82
covalent bonds 9, 11, 21, 62, 63
covalent substances 11, 62, 63
cracking hydrocarbons 20
crinkly bits 51
crocodile 51
crude oil 17, 18, 21
crust 40, 49, 50, 52, 53
cryolite 26
crystal 10
crystallisation 13
crystallize 47
crystals 13, 48, 49, 61
cuboid 10
cyanide 15

Index

D

dangerous 19
decay 17, 44
deforestation 43
density 1, 24, 28, 50, 58, 59, 76
diamond 11, 23, 71
diesel 18, 20
diffusion experiments 4
dilute acid 73
displacement reactions 33, 74
dissolving 4, 10, 25, 34, 35, 40, 41, 60
distillation 13, 14
Dmitri 37, 55
double bonds 21, 22
drinking water 31
dyes 13, 66

E

Earth 40, 43, 46, 49, 50
earthquakes 50, 52, 53
Earth's magnetic field 50, 53
earthworm 51
easy marks 12
easy peasy 13, 36
electric wiring 28, 76
electrical conductors 25
electrical discharge tubes 58
electricity 27, 35
electrodes 26
electrolysis 23, 25, 26, 35, 64, 72
electrolytes 27, 35
electron shells 8, 57
electrons 6-10, 27, 55-59
elements 7, 10, 12, 13, 36, 37, 55-57
end of civilisation as we know it... 18
endothermic reactions 33, 86
energy 19
energy level diagrams 87
energy levels 8
enzyme 83, 84
equations 34
erosion and transport 45, 46
ethane 21
ethene 20-22
eutrophication 31
evaporation 2, 5, 13, 45, 64
evidence 51, 53
evolution 41, 47
exothermic reactions 31, 33, 86
expansion 1, 45
expensive 26
experiment 39
explosion 78
extrusive igneous rocks 46, 49

F

faulty gas fires 19
fermentation 84
fertilisers 30, 31, 69
fiery abyss 46
filter paper 13
filtration 13
fire risk 19
fish, death of 31, 42, 66
five lab tests 15
fizzing 60
flame 61
flammable 15, 19
flat spots 3
flooding 43
fluorine 60, 62, 65
food 64, 83, 84
forces of attraction 1, 2
formulae 34, 37
fossil fuels 17, 40, 42
fossils 47, 49, 51
fractional distillation 14, 18, 20
fractionating column 14, 18
francium 59
free electrons 70
freezing 3, 45, 64, 83
fuels 18, 33, 86
full shells 8, 9, 56-58
fume cupboard 62
funnel 13

G

galvanising 75
gas 2, 17, 34, 62
gas room heaters 19
gas syringe 39, 78, 80, 81
gases 1, 4, 11, 12, 58
get shot 8
giant covalent structures 11
giant ionic structures 10, 61
giant structure 70
glass 29, 65
gloopy liquids 20
glowing splint 15
gold 23, 72, 73
good conductors 76
goodness' sake 7
granite 46, 49
graphite 11, 26, 71
graphs 3, 80
green plants 40
greenhouse effect 43
gripping stuff 31
groups 8, 56, 58, 59, 62

H

Haber process 30
haematite 23, 24
half equations 35
halogens 62, 65
harmful 15
harmful rays 41
hazard symbols 15
HCl 5, 35, 62, 63, 65, 66, 67, 68, 69, 80, 81, 85
heat 27, 33, 46
heat and pressure 48
heat energy 2
heating graph 3
helium 36, 58
hideously unattractive 29
Himalayas 52
hydro-electric power station 27
hydrocarbons 18-20
hydrochloric acid 5, 35, 62, 63, 65-69 80, 81, 85
hydrogen 15, 25, 30, 60, 64, 65, 67, 72, 73, 80
hydrogen peroxide 81
hydroxides 60, 68, 73

I

ice 45, 64
ice caps melting 43
Iceland 53
identifying rocks 47, 49
igneous rocks 46, 49
impurities 24
in your dreams 24
incomplete combustion 19
India 51, 52
industrial activity 39
industrial reactions 82
inert gases 58
inks 13, 14
inter-molecular forces 11
intrusive igneous rocks 46, 49
iodine 60, 62, 63, 65
ionic bonds and compounds 9, 10, 35, 59, 61, 62, 65
ions 6, 9, 10, 11, 27, 35
iron 12, 24, 28, 33, 50, 53, 63, 67, 70, 72-76, 82
iron nail 74, 75
iron ore 23, 24
iron oxide 23, 24, 33
iron powder 12
iron sulphide 12
iron(III) bromide 63
irritant 15
isotopes 7
it tastes horrid 14

Index

J

jerky movement 4
jet fuel 18, 20
jigsaw fit 51

K

keep trying 24
kerosine 18, 20
kinda scary 38
krypton 58

L

lab tests 15
lactic acid 84
lactose 84
lasers 58
lattice 1
lead 23, 72
learn and enjoy 6, 19, 28, 63,
    71, 73
learn stuff 2
learn the boring facts 62
light bulbs 58
lime 66
limestone 24, 29, 42, 44-48
limewater 15, 69
liquids 1, 4, 11, 14, 34, 62
lithium 59, 60
litmus paper 15
lot of practice 34
lubricating oil 20

M

magma 46, 48, 49, 51-53
magnesium 23, 33, 67, 72, 80
magnesium oxide 66
magnetic 50
magnetic "stripes" 51
malachite 23
malleable 70
manganese 76
mantle 50
marble 46, 48
marble chips 80
margarine 65
mass 6, 7, 37
mass balance 78, 80
mass number 7, 36
matter 1
measure, speed of a reaction 78
mega-death 31
melting 2, 10
melting points 10, 11, 26
mercury 71
metal halides 63

metal ore 23
metallic bonds 70
metallic crystal structure 70
metals 10, 28, 56, 59,
    63, 70, 72-76
metamorphic rocks 46, 48
meteorites 50
methane 21, 30, 40
mica 48
microscope 4, 6
mid-Atlantic ridge 51, 53
milk 84
Millom 24
minerals 23, 48, 49
mixtures 4, 12, 18
molecular substances 11, 62, 63
molecules
    1, 2, 4, 11, 18, 19, 20, 35, 62
molten 10, 24, 26, 35
monatomic 58
moonshine 14
Mount Everest 52
mountains 51, 52, 53
M$_r$ (Relative Formula Mass) 36,
    37
mudstone 47, 48

N

NaCl 35
naptha 18
natural gas 17, 30, 44
negatively charged 6
neon 58
neutral atoms 6, 35
neutral salts 31, 60
neutralisation 29, 31, 33, 66, 68,
    86
neutrons 6, 7
Newlands' Octaves 55
nickel 50, 70, 76
nitrates 31
nitric acid 31, 42, 67-69, 82
nitrogen 12, 30, 39, 40, 42, 82
nitrogen dioxide 68
nitrogen monoxide 31
nitrogen oxides 42, 67
no charge 6
noble de-use 58
noble gases 39, 40, 58
non-metal oxides 68
non-metals 10, 62, 71
non-porous rock 17
nothing dafter 50
notorious "squeaky pop" 15, 60, 67
nucleus 6-8

O

ocean floor 51
oceanic plate 52
oceanic trench 52
oceans 40, 41, 43
octane 20
odourless 19
oil 17, 18, 44
old rogue 37, 55, 77
olden days 54
opposite charges 9
orbits 6
ores 23, 25, 26
organisms 41
outer shell 8, 9, 57, 58
outsmart them 7
oxidation 33
oxides 23, 28, 61, 68, 73, 75
oxidising 15, 31
oxygen 8, 12, 15, 19, 39,
    40, 42, 82
ozone layer 41, 42

P

"Pangaea" 51
paraffin 20
particles 6
party balloons 58
percentage mass 37
% of oxygen in the air 39
Periodic Table 8, 36, 55, 56
pestle and mortar 13
petrol 15, 18, 19, 20, 82
pH indicator 60, 66
pH scale 66
photographic film 65
photosynthesis 44, 86
physical state 34
pipes, copper 28
plants 45
plastics 18, 20, 22
plate tectonics 50-52
platinum 72
platinum catalyst 31, 82
poisonous 19, 62
pollen grains 4
polyethene, polythene 22
polymers 22
porous rocks 17
positive charge 6
potassium 8, 23, 59-61, 72, 73
potassium manganate(VII) 4
power stations 42
precipitate 33, 63, 78
pressure 1, 22, 30, 46, 79

Index

pressure and heat 17
products 78, 85, 87
propane 21
proper motor cars 22
protein 83
protons 6, 7, 55
pure water 14
purifying 26

Q
quartz 23
quicklime 29

R
radioactive decay 50
radon 58
rain 45, 68
rapid random motion 1, 4
rates of reaction 78
raw material 18
reactants 33, 78, 85, 87
reaction rates 79
reactivity 59, 62
reactivity series 23, 72
real simple 6
reduction 23, 24, 25, 33, 72
Relative Atomic Mass, A_r 36, 37, 55
Relative Formula Mass, M_r 36
relative mass 7
respiration 44
reversible reactions 30, 33, 82, 85
road building/surfacing 24, 29
Rock Cycle 46
rock salt 13, 64
rock strata 51
rocks 45-51
roots 45
rubidium 59
rusting 28, 75, 78

S
salt 10, 13, 64, 66-68
salts 35, 47, 60, 63
San Andreas Fault 53
San Francisco 53
sand 11, 13, 24, 29, 64
sandstone 17, 47
scary stuff 36
schist 48
"sea" of free electrons 70
sea shells 29, 44, 47, 48
sea water 14, 41
sediment 17, 46, 47, 52
sedimentary rocks 29, 40, 46, 47

seismic waves 50
separation techniques 13, 14
shale 47
sharing electrons 9
shells, electrons 6, 8
sigh 22, 28, 36
silicates 29
silicon 71
silicon dioxide 11, 23, 24, 29
silver 72, 73
silver halides 63, 65
silver nitrate 63, 74
slag 24
slaked lime 29
slate 48
sleep 19, 31, 37
sludge 25
smelters 27
smile and enjoy 7
smoke particles 4, 19
smoky yellow flame 19
soda 29
sodium 8, 23, 37, 59, 60, 72, 73
sodium carbonate 29, 37, 65, 69
sodium chloride 64
sodium hydrogencarbonate 65
sodium hydroxide 64, 65
sodium thiosulphate 81
solids 1, 2, 14, 34, 62
Solvay process 65
sooty marks 19
South America 51, 52
speed of reaction 67, 82
"squeaky pop" 15, 60, 67
stainless steel 28
state symbols 34
states of matter 1
statues 29, 42
steam 40, 41
steel 28, 70
stuff on atoms 6
stuff or not 16
stupid 19
subduction zone 52
sugar 84
sulphur 12, 42, 81
sulphur dioxide 42, 68
sulphur impurities 42
sulphuric acid 15, 42, 67-69
Sun 42, 43, 45, 64
surface area 80, 82
swamps 17
swapping electrons 9
symbols 34

symmetrical pattern 51, 53

T
tar 20
tarnish 72
tectonic plates 52, 53
temperature 3
the name of the game, pal... 8
thermal decomposition 20, 33, 85, 86
thermometer 14
timeless mysteries 6
tin 23, 70
tiny 6
toxic 15
transition metals 55, 76, 82
transport 45
trench 52
trends 59, 62
turn blue 31
two simple numbers 7

U
universal indicator 66
unreactive 25
upshot 7
UV rays 42

V
vapours 19, 62
vibrate 1, 2
viscous 19, 50
volatile 19
volcanoes 40, 46, 49, 52, 53
volume 39

W
water 4, 15, 19, 21, 25, 30, 60
water pipes 76
water vapour 39, 40
weathering 45, 46
wee joke 78
well keen 8

X
xenon 58

Y
yeast 84
yoghurt 84

Z
zinc 23, 67, 72, 73-76
"zup" 27
zymase 84